Time Curtain

By

S. Egroeg Reklaw

ISBN: 1-4033-5598-3 (e-book)
ISBN: 1-4033-5599-1 (Paperback)

This book is printed on acid free paper.

1stBooks - rev. 10/03/02

DEDICATION

This book is especially dedicated to May Hilda Smith.

To all the people who have touched my life, especially in the early days on the Brunswick Avenue and at the old Crescent School. In remembering the youthful days with George Walker, Glen Wilson, Alvin Richards, Selvyn Byfield, Seymour "Jack" Smith and all the other friendly guys who laughed, swam in the rivers and canals after we played cricket and football throughout the summers of so long ago.

And to the Matriarchs (Rosa Jones, Dolly Cox, Myrtle Jones) and the Patriarchs (Vinton Jones, Daniel Smith, Joseph Smith, Granville Smith) of the family who stood their grounds, kept the space for spiritual calmness and made all this fun possible... A salute to Bev McKoy for her friendship over the years, not withstanding my teasing her about the salutation of enigmatic "Hindi."

A special thanks to Grace Parkis for her numerous help in editing this book although the phrases were ever so foreign to her.

Table of Contents

CHAPTER 1

"FULL CIRCLE?"

Wilton Shadows, (Mr. Wilton Shadows…) returned home to live in the district of *Am Steady,* where he tried blending in with the village people. Now, here he is at this local outdoors concert standing in the evening shadows, away from the raucous gathering of people near the preparation of mouth watering jerk food. The jovial undulating voices shout in the local patois as each person competes to be heard over the blaring music being played from the throbbing bass-emphasized reggae systems. One fellow across the street was playing oldies in front of his bar. The other sound system up the street could merely be heard, but it was beating out some of the new craze dance music, or according to the younger set, *Dance Hall* music. Shadows watched the scene, being aware he was also being watched. Most things here were being done with him in mind. It was done to impress and to show him, the stranger, that the locals are not some out of the way country bumpkins. He was impressed. Men were getting into fake arguments to show they can trade words… the women were shouting in their loud siren voices in a mock show of feminine competition. The jerk seller continues preparing his stuff, pandering to his customers with biting witticism… one woman showed a great interest in roving her eyes at the Shadows; she had a problem being discreet…she was pretty too…perhaps always winning her game in this small village. It was too obvious she has a motive…when Shadows moved towards her back she ignored her conversational group, especially the man to whom she was speaking, and made almost a complete turn to make eye contact with Shadows. Their eyes met, but the contrived unawareness in his eyes did not fool her. She again pressed for more recognition; she would not be denied… Shadows openly stared her down. She smiles and shifted her gaze, but not her attention towards a companion who was desperately trying to command her attention. Shadows had been at many village scenes similar to this one. He smiled in recognition of years gone by; of being reminded of the explosive mixture of a pretty damsel and a village dance. He recollects that dangerous situation when he and his buddies from the city made a dance in a very popular village. He nearly got injured then when he chooses not to follow his instincts when a very pretty girl wantonly threw herself at him. She informed him there was a separation with her boyfriend during the day. Now, no one should be considered separated over the course of one day. Young people have these romantic notions of *making u*p during the nights, especially in the darkness. He walked away in the darkness from his city protective group within the company of this lady and her friends…he was no longer living in this community…his roots were there, but he was specifically unknown to the boyfriend and his two nervous friends who now wanted to hurt him. They cornered Shadows, blocking his exit towards his friends. As the discussion moved towards an uncompromising argument the boyfriend produced a knife. His two friends were unwilling associates. They knew the danger, and they were near to the Police Station also. With no escape, Shadows couldn't get to his friends and too proud or too foolish to run the other way, his antagonists slowly closed the distance between them. The glistening of the deadly blade in the light of the dimly lit bulb from a distant street light tells him he was in deadly peril. Just then he heard the sound of a motor cycle and sees the headlamp casting a bright yellowish light on the back of his antagonists. He wished it was his big aggressive in-law, but oh no; it was the lamb of the family, his womanizing friend John. He knew they were in trouble fighting these guys, but he was still glad to see him. John had on a brown riding coat. It made him look bigger in the darkness. When he came off the bike he slightly stumbles. He was slightly inebriated and the bike was slightly too heavy for him. He was also not a very competent rider either. He parked immediately beside the guy with the knife. Shadows was quickly trying to warn him, but the spirited and brave John took the ascendancy in the conflict. Someone must have told him there was trouble…he straightened up to a couple inches above his normal height and started a tirade of curses *that he possibly will have to return to prison again, although after his long sentence he promised his family he would not kill anybody else*. Shadows instantly realized his friend was bluffing his way as a dangerous long-term criminal. A brilliant ruse by a quiet man to save a careless friend! The guy with the knife shuffled his feet backwards as John moved closer, threateningly put his hand in his coat pocket asking, "Who mi kill first now…" The boyfriend

3

became calm and his other two friends were totally pacified. They were now tugging at the boyfriend's sleeve begging him to leave. John raucously asked, "We a go fight now or not? If we nah go fight then we gone!" No one wants the confrontation so we discreetly rode away. As they rode away to safety he remembers still trembling at John's closeness to the guy's knife. Shadows recognized without John's close contact with danger the boyfriend probably would have believed John was just bluffing. In retrospect, Shadows realizes that John actually put his life on the line to save his. Most people then had some type of a weapon, and the weapon of choice was knife. *Shadows never travel with weapon.* In the city the bad women had what is called *a tenge lance.* To exhibit the *"bad gal"* image she would have to carry it in her bosom the ease of instant accessibility. The more sober types kept it safely among the clothes in their grip—to be used in time of conflict. The country people claimed that such weapons were only carried by "de bad gal dem a town;" they have no use for it because they will "back dem 'lass"—use their cutlasses.

Those were the days before Shadows and his motor cycle buddies ride with The EL GROUP. He now momentarily closed his eyes and segues to another more carefree time, a simpler time before being engulfed with life's social branding. A type of branding, which tends to erode ones spiritual will to enjoy the simpler life. Shadows reminisced about his old buddies: El Roy and "Happy," peace brothers! El Zeig, El Bial, El Zabalu, Tumdek and the rest of the fun loving bunch. He recalled numerous occasions "prowling" with El Rups, the ingenious "Rude Boy."

He remembered the night when they "checked" out a hairdresser in one of the seamy spots in their town. In those days one could easily meet ones Waterloo in the narrow dark lanes. But there they stood immobile in the darkness; just wishing and hoping to favorable attract her attention and make a civil contact. In the darkness *under the spreading mango tree* she emerged, with one glaring light bulb strung from a mango tree at her back. In the doorway they had a glance of her not so old grandmother preparing for bed. The young beautiful hairdresser tossed out her cat and taunted in her whispering voice, *"A pussy you want, see one ya!"* This was not too comfy an area either. Apparently, the pretty girl was tired; she had just returned from working at her shop. Or possibly she had just decided to change friends...or did not wish any type of romantic interlude when her grandma was around. Take your pick of the excuses! Anyway, El Rups seems to have this outrageous personal "handshakes" with the ladies. It was the same El Rups that another woman delicately pushed into the sea at Gunboat Beach, to either sink or swim. We were just lucky that Shadows taught El Rups to swim some weeks before that frightening episode. Again, the same El Rups visited another woman; in the darkness an affable policeman emerge from her room. The woman hinted to El Rups she was pregnant... It appears he wanted her to give the baby to the *other* man, which she did. But then again who said the child was ever his! El Rups went to another dimension in another situation by activating the power of suggestion. He gave his girl friend Glauber Salt as a birth control because she inquired how none of his sisters were never pregnant.

It seems he viewed her questioning him as a personal attack on his family's privacy. Apparently it worked because there were no offspring. From that time onward the El Group started using the word El Rups, "*di dawg!*" In those days there were numerous housewife tales about birth controls…none were really effective. It was during those years when Shadows met the young speed king "Souse di Back," otherwise known as "Souse di," because after hearing the long label with its history, everyone generally gets a shorter, friendlier and more acceptable version of their nickname. One can imagine if a friend is "named," *Bawly-Bawly* because of his crying behaviors in the early *A-classes*—first grader school days. By the time he reaches the middle grades and before he is "out school" he would be finally known as "Bawler." Everyone around him will finally call him "baller" on the playing field. The historicity of his earlier childhood behaviors will be lost to his new friends as they gets into perceptibility issues…he is now a school hero who skillfully works the ball against the oppositions. Anyway, Souse di's riding friend had this astonishing idea that "sousing the back" –bathing in the canal, by jumping in the water backwards, thereby hitting the water with your back could be an effective birth control! He had the numbers to prove it too.

CHAPTER 2

TIME RESONANCE

Shadows recollected what in those days were called "living in the woods" with his parents—living far from the villages or towns. The solitary woods were rife with dangerous sinkholes. It was said the land was a legacy to the females of the family. Apparently the females' legacies were to be in the woods, whereas the males were given the more attractive lands on the main roads that were more accessible in the village. Sounds contrary, but this gender-type decision was made by another woman, their mother! Shadows recalls the dreadful experience of once wandering in a cave full of bats. He was always wandering around, being lonely as the only child at home when everyone else went home or whenever the parents are late from an appointment. He remembers an occasion when no one was at home. This had never happened before! His mother or father was always there when he comes from school. His loneliness overcame him, and he seeks companionship in a fowl coop near the house…all domesticated animals can be comforting when one is lonely. An animal can be a comfort in your loneliness in the dark, not so with plants. Plants became more like mysterious entities, like watchful sinister silhouettes in the dark that engulfs you with a feeling of helplessness with their lack of mobility and vocal responses. They just stood there watching but physically and, or emotionally unwilling to respond. Then any sounds trees make become eerie and confusing or considered to be so if you are already in a state of frightful distress. While walking he asks himself why he is remembering this incident… But of course he knew why. His return has rekindled the spiritual love for his homeland and the parents he love. Now he is at this mental movie replaying all these prior events long before his mother's transition. Their last Earthly interaction is an indelible event that is easily accessed with refreshed clarity over all these years. He can still clearly *"sees"* his mother faintly raising her head to deliver her last Earthly family message. At that time Shadows thought it was the beginning of the end for his existence. He quietly watched his mother's unsuccessful effort in commanding her weak unsteady neck to faithfully hold her bobbing head. As a last resort she propped herself on her right shoulder, and crooked her arm while trying to steady her swaying head with her trembling right hand. She peered through the glass window amidst white bedclothes with her white, deathly glazed tear filled eyes, and pronounced in a faint, halting and whispering voice that her end is near. Shadows still remember the pre-death spectacle, and is reminded of the foolish little bureaucratic starchy, white clad nurse's command, telling them she is "…badly sick," so no one is allowed in the room until she recovers; "let her sleep now." Perhaps she should have ended her little speech with "please don't awake me…" The nurses' intentions may be good, but her decision then to put a barrier between a dying person and their family was incorrect…

Shadows vividly remembered the events during that time, which he now called the *deathwatch*. Everything then was in a state of flux: her breathing and appearance, the family's weeping voices, the billowing white curtains, the slowly moving nurses who deliberately watched and fiddled with little insignificant things in the background... Everything changes except one thing...she just continued peering through the window with her glazed eyes, peering steadfastly searching in his direction. He stood there and remained silent, but she would not be denied, she held her wobbly head, and just gazed unflinchingly in his direction with her deathly white glazed eyes, focusing as if imaging the last snapshot while on a passing train. He helplessly watched ...and silently listened. He now realized he was seeing the final curtain between life and death...

When told that her son was there too, she uncharacteristically broke down, and sadly weeps for the very last time, while in a tired and halting voice imploring her attentive audience, her friends and relatives to please protect her *last heritage*. It must have taken an enormous amount of physical strength to make that last vocal request. She must have summoned her final iota of mobile energy from deep within her inner core to communicate that last farewell. "I'll have to sleep now, I am going to die!" Shadows vividly recalled his premonition of death while on a quiet school road. "What happens if my mother should die now!" he asked no one in particular. He is still wondering and seeking a closure to, "Why asked that question when it was never contemplated?" How can he ever forget his mother telling the group, "No, I am

not coming home…I will not see you here again!"
Premonition someone said is ones ability to decode the
ethereal energy signatures that permeates the Cosmos.
Was this a case? The question of his mother's death
was never contemplated but was earnestly repeated as
if a message was delivered. He was besides an
electrical transformer station when that message
occurs. He never knew that such premonition was to
forever transform his life. He now understood it as a
communiqué on a higher plane of consciousness…not
to be trivialized with simple electrical impulses. At
least he hopes so. His mother's departure really
brought on diverse stages of uncertainty and an
unbelieving sense of loss. The loss opened a different
line of cooperation and communication between family
members. He sees it more as Friends eternal…a
cooperative family community project that finds love
where there was mere indifference.

On reflecting on his mother's last rites, he
remembered the exact spot he saw her face for the last
time. It was at this spot where his boyhood friend The
Sprinkler made his raucous stance against an
imaginary ghost. Shadows and his friends always taunt
him about how his uncle, Mass Burty fooled him by
playing the ghost… This time the uncle who played the
ghost was crying for real. He lost himself rolling on the
floor, and refused to be comforted. The man has just
lost his wife, and his long time friend. We all stood
there and openly weep. One silently weeps for a
mother, other distraught family members for a sister
and others for a departed friend.

Then there was this "Former Other" who openly
re-visited his life with his vanishing lover, and quite

possibly was second guessing his behaviors with a prick of conscience… The "Former Other" had passed on emotional distress to this dead woman in the earlier days. He was very eloquent while speaking to the spirit of the departed: "If the body can hear me, I am here with the goodness of spirit. This visit is in peace…" He meant well as he stooped, took off his expensive cap and spoke his piece in peace in a clear and commanding voice intermingled with emotions. He looked sincere and open, but then was it too late. Now there was no vibrant voice to grant him absolution. The gathering became silent as he spoke; they knew the history of his story. During the night he sings his *setup songs* until daybreak, and then finally moved away tired and at peace the next morning. Shadows became the wiser too for that single experience…Shadows watched the proceedings and noticed the Orator never came over to pay his respect or condolences to the "Dearly Departed's" family. He was one of them too; did he not know that? The eyes of a child looked at the adults then and marveled at their aloofness. Now he knows that is the way such people live… It seems that there were earlier miscommunications, but what can you expect; this is an island with very poor communication skills. The lesson learnt that day was human temperament and impermanence…so talk to us while we are still alive and able to converse; don't wait to mumble your wish list at our grave sites!

Like the "Former Other," now, Shadows will never be able to tell her of his experiences, the way he felt about the numerous Sundays they spent together in his childhood. He remembers her preparing those special Sunday morning breakfasts. Shadows always think his father's food was better. It was so long ago, but he still remembers the remarkable dish his father prepared that Christmas morning. Honestly, the man could cook! He also recollected the stranger woman who came to lunch one summer. She ate his father's entire portion of food although she claimed not liking the food. When she left, his father wondered aloud, "... if she likes it, what would she do next?" He recalls his dad pouring the rest of his lemonade out the window in mild disgust. She drank from his mug after finishing her glass, and then excused herself from the table and left in the broiling sun. People were very private then; never drink from others utensils even if they politely gave their consents! You will often hear the excuse: "*No, make every body die with their own disease...*" The joke is; Shadows later had a similar experience with two lady guests. One was invited to dinner. She brought a friend. They both ate all the food without leaving him a morsel! In fairness to the invited guest, she did make an effort to leave him some. Her friend's mood immediately changed to one of displeasure. On seeing the gloom of displeasure crossing her face Shadows immediately gave his consent to their *total* eating pleasure. It is disconcerting how certain unpleasant events have a tendency to repeat themselves in a family.

Anyway, his mother's food preparation was very different. Shadows liked the food but he dread the preparations when she would get into her serious command moods, and sternly played the parent by sending him for plates to set the table. How could he forget the type of table setting dialogue?

"Bring me a bread plate, please." Shadows remembers there were always that strong pause, and her unnerving stare before the word, *please.* Then after that all the unnerving regimented, socializing, and table-setting hell breaks loose. "No, that is a saucer…I need a bread plate. Now go and bring me the right plate, and try not to break it because it is in my family for years." It was never *our* family. She once enlightened him that it is not his family because, my grandmother, "Mummaw" is my relative and not my family. She then confused him more by telling him that as his mother, and his family; she had never given him a plate. In other words don't break it because it is not yours I got it from your relative, which is not your family… Bring me a teaspoon. I said teaspoon. Why are you bringing me a tablespoon? I said to bring me a cup, why are you coming with a mug? You don't understand me anymore?" Shadows remembers when he did not answer she would calmly ask if he did not hear the question. Now he has to reply because that was a direct question. It was not as if she was just talking to herself. He would then pause and answer, "Yes mom," or perhaps he would answer "No mom." If he said yes, she would ask why he did not carry out her order. This one answer could be very tricky. He now believes it shows defiance. This answer may call for a certain safe distance between them, just to be safe of course. One never knows! This is where she would ask if *she has horn why he is standing so far.* If she gives a serious look when this question is asked you better give a reply. Of course the reply would have to be no! That is a no-brainer. He always wonders what she would do if he answered otherwise. Even now he chuckled about that response. He once challenged her authority when he swept the yard and asked where to put the garbage. She pointed towards her mouth…in his subdued anger; he cautiously mimicked walking towards her… She became catatonic, quiet and a bit confused! His only one challenging moment to her authority, and he lives to tell the tale without pain too.

Now, if the answer to her "You don't understand me anymore" is no, then she may stop whatever she is doing; give him that special *"have you lost a scre*w" look, sighs and then shakes her head as if resigning herself to having an autistic child. During all this discussion her voice was always low and precise. It must have been her Sunday mode. There were never shouting… Shadows never told his friends about this Sunday ritual, or the command to wash plates. His friends would possibly laugh him out of the Village for doing "dem gal pickney work!" Even now he cannot understand how they could have repeated this same ritual so often, and he still forgot which utensil is which. Perhaps she was right when she said, "You romped out all the information out of your head!"

He remembered her picking coffee during one of those cool early mornings. She told him it was his duty to pick up the "rat-cut-coffee" under those *"crawny"*— messy trees. She kept on repeating that it would buy his Christmas gift at some place in town calls the Grand Market. In his child's mind he pictures this *"grand market"* as a busy and beautiful place with diverse colors; that was until she mentioned about the prowling *"masquerade"* or *"John Canoe"* bands with "prancing devils" with their sharp three-pronged forks. According to her, you will have to appease this frightful fork wielding "devil" by tossing him money on the ground. He had no money, and never did, so he immediately lost his interest in the grand market. As a child he thought that picking up the *rat-cut* coffee was the worst thing that could ever happen to him. On looking back now, Shadows realizes that was his first real duty as a child. He was surprised when he realized she really meant for him to do it. There would be no playing. It was in this same area where he tried outrunning her. He went visiting against her ruling while she was absent. She came for him. She was furious but pleasant to her hosts, although she openly warned him of what was going to happen to him. He then foolishly waited for her to finish her conversation with her friend before trying to run home. That was such an infant mistake. Shadows learnt quickly after that whenever you transgressed a parent's rule, you should try *keeping a wide circle* from them.

She taught him so many things even to build slingshots and fly kites. He had the first "*tissue paper*"—multi-colored paper kite among the whole family and villagers in his community. When his school friends from the adjoining district of West Prospect told him that the bigger boys have kite wars; using razor blades on the tails of their kites to cut other kites intruding in their space. He thought it was a good idea. He told her about it. She looked at him as if to say, "I have created a monster here." He knew she did not give him the kite as a war machine. She quietly said, "You are the only one flying kite out there. The razor blade will cut your own kite, and it may fly across the river to Prospect." She then laughed and walked away. In his child's mind, he saw his beautiful kite erratically drifting away, far up in the clouds after being cut by his own razor blade…it was just fluttering in the wind hopelessly out of his reach, way across the river to one of those bigger boys in West Prospect…

She showed him how to use sounds to *revive* stunned chickens by beating a pan over the chicken's head, and how to get rid of "*setting hens*" when they have "*laid out their lots,*" and have had no eggs to sit on. This is where you use a small portion of water to douse the hen. She told him to be very careful with the water treatment, and never to dip the hen in the water because she once did that as a child and killed an irate neighbor's fowl. In truthfulness Shadows believe that neither of these methods was too effective, although on one occasion he saw the "revival" method works. As they say, everything takes time… It was so contrary with all these fowls around, but she did not eat chicken. It took Shadows years to know this. Imagine being told that chickens are nasty, while spitting in disgust with the appropriate wry face to show her disapproval… "Pyack!" It must have been an emotional battle for her to clean and cooked a "nasty" chicken to feed the family. No wonder she is always sitting away from the table with her calabash dish of spiced calaloo (greens) and salted fish whenever chicken is prepared. It seems that no one generally ever ask a mother if she enjoys the meal being prepared; how selfish.

But it was in another Village that Shadows finally learned to kill birds by trapping them in a tree with what he called a *chokey*. When he pulled the cord the bird started suffocating and fluttering. He had expected it to escape. They usually do! It did not; it died. He finally caught one of them. Then he found out it was not enjoyable. There is no fun in it this time. It generally was so much fun when it escapes; then he would point skywards and joyfully shouts, "*I will catch you next time bird.*" Death is too final! It ends without sounds and movements too. Although he had never caught any bird this way he decided then, it would be better using a *callaban*—an open-ended pyramid-shaped enclosure trap that is elevated off the ground by sticks. At least the bird would be alive, and he has a choice of releasing it. Shadows plainly recollects raiding a nest in their tangerine tree for two baby birds. The mother bird eventually flew down into captivity, to certain death with food for its hungry young. This was an early lesson learnt about sacrifice and love. A mother's love for her babies, although one cannot ascertain if it was a male bird. It should have been a parent's love, but most males were never seen to exhibit this level of personal awareness towards their children, unless the parent is a *centered* Rastafarian. Not even towards their daughters whom they try to grow up as little ladies. Some males were protective of their daughters, while most females were very protective of their sons. At this time Shadows has no intention of complicating this simple tale with some complicated and nasty Oedipus psychological gender-preferential ramblings. He never heard about Freud then… The males were always told to be rough and tough. Many parents were never keen on emphasizing any form of intellectual exercise…over the generations we have seen the result of such lack of tutelage.

Once, Shadows and his mom were returning from the fields. He had a very slight bundle. (There were always those mumbling but very private remarks of not giving their sons heavy loads. It seems that doing so could result in some woman in the son's later life complaining about *"your man's back."* He never understood the rationale but a certain cultural common sense warned him never to ask. Similar to a woman not damaging any man, or else he belongs to you for life...) It was very hot and they stopped at her Indian friend for a drink of water. The lady kindly handed water to his mother who had a basket on her head. She puts the water to her lips and then stopped as if violently restrained. Her fiery eyes were staring at him from under her broad rimmed straw hat; questioning him with an intensity he has never before observed. He looks at her and smiled an appeasement gesture, wondering what is happening. She brusquely said, "Here, you drink it first." He paused, a long indecisive pause emanating from his cultural confusion. Remembers this; the concept of "drinking first " was a sign of individual power. A child has no power then in that society. He gladly drank, but with reservation; perhaps like the biblical Abraham making the decision to lay prone on a sacrificial altar. In those days when a mother says, "drink" you drink, end of story. "There could be *no long argument*...!" On the way home he asked why did she let him *drink first*? She told him the story of the thirsty travelers, a mother and a son. The mother got the water and drank it. When she was finished, and tried handing it to the child, he was laying dead at her feet. He died of thirst. She became nasty telling him that while the woman was there *gwapping*—ravenously drinking the water, the child die of thirst. Shadows remember her feeling sorry for

18

the child, but her view was, "we can't trust unoo." That is parents can't trust children as children will do things to their parents resulting in *dem* (government) *come haul and pull you!* He was shocked because he never knew that the *dem*, the government cares about children too. He has never seen any of the "them" either. Now he always smiles when he realized his mother was furious at the child for dying, and thereby placed his mother, another woman in trouble. If it were not so tragic it would have been hilarious; his mother was the very first feminist he met. He knew she missed having a daughter. She had never openly voiced the opinion, but many times she implied that girls were better than boys were. She always equates her preference to a girl child's behavior. But it seems she was more concern about her golden age. She rightfully espoused the notion that a man goes away with his wife and forgets his old and indigent mother. A woman has a different sense of value; one that is generally more nurturing. In this way she is more prone to help her old mother. Shadows at this time knew such to be true. Her disturbing comment then was, "You can't get an ole frock to wear from a man!" He remembers disliking that frock comment. Men don't generally wear frocks during those times. Do they now? With all her grumbling she has never eased her care towards him in the slightest. As a child he asked her why she is grumbling about certain things, she snapped that she has "*to give vents to her feelings*!" That was scary, because in those days you just do not question them. He got lucky that time and he knew never to do that again. Quite likely she was waiting for him to dare and question her just one more time. Some of her greatest joys were visiting her only sister whom has many daughters. Once she hoisted one of her sister's baby daughters, paused and then looked straight into Shadows' eyes. He remembered there was a deep sense of love there that he had never seen except on her deathbed at the hospital when someone mentioned he was there. When their eyes met then there were questions on a different plane. He was right beside her holding onto her dress, and she was just outrageously playing with the baby… throwing it up in the air, cooing with it, coddling it, laughing loudly, and just behaving as any other little girl with a brand new baby doll. A few moments later, she calm down, stopped and looked down at him. He thinks she forgets him and had just recognized that there is a problem. When she looked down at him her eyes opened wide as if seeing something for the first time. She then calmly asked if he wanted to hold the baby; knowing very well that he would refuse. When he refused; she slowly and quietly handed the baby to her sister. Her face was serene as if infused by an Inner Light. For years Shadows wonders about that incident. He never asked her about it. But over the years he knew why. She was extremely attached to one of her nieces. That was a good choice too. She apparently sensed the innate strength and honesty within this niece. She avoids causing a conflict of ownership between her son and her niece. It was years later, while in his early teens he recognized the deep attachment his mother had for girls. He recalled the meeting of his mom and his cousin on a lonely railway track. He still "hears" his cousin's piercing voice as she runs down the tracks, calling his mom's name and the reaction he saw on his mother's face when she could not ascertain where the sound originates. His cousin's urgent high pitched voice came wailing down the railroad tracks, as if she was being chased by their childish idea of death, the imaginary primary school bogeyman, called the Catcher Man. He recalled his mothers' welcoming reaction towards her niece as he stood there watching them exchanging greetings as we looked across the green pastures from the meandering steel tracks. Our discussions were warm, but very basic without being feebly elementary…unknown to us that day was to be our last meeting.

In the earlier time, prior to the railroad track meeting, his mom had another younger niece visiting from the city. This one was pretty but quite noisy, contrary and the spookiest infant cousin he can recall. His mom called her "Rock and Tawny," because she is always rocking herself to sleep. The child scared the entire district by claiming to be seeing all types of *duppies* in every nook and cranny. Shadows then wondered if they had *duppies* in the bright and pretty town because he always associates ghosts with darkness.

Shadows remembers that the rule of talking with parents were to be very careful of the questions you could ask? The villagers had always have dogs at home. And there were always mongoose lurking to get a chicken. On one such occasion, there was a commotion and the fowls became alarmed. His mother shouted, "Mongoose!" During that time they had a big, pretty, and playful brown puppy at home. The other dogs, especially Laggo was very old so no one actually bothers him. His mother pointed into the direction of the mongoose. The pup rushes with great speed in the pointed direction. Perhaps he thinks this was one of his mother's playful fetching exercises. Instantly, the dog rushed back screaming towards her, with the mongoose at its heels. That frightened dog hid under the bed until it was dark. That friendly puppy was eventually named Joslyn. The name was not ever meant to denigrate Shadows' childish nemesis. It was given by some of the older guys that usually visit Shadows' home. The aftermath of that *"mongoose incident"* almost caused serious disciplinary incident for Shadows. He laughed and asked her why people are always calling, "Mongoose" whenever mongoose is in the vicinity. She paused and calmly looks at him. She was waiting for him to fully explain. Shadows smiles, and then boldly said, "When people say mongoose, are they calling for the mongoose to come to them?" Oh, heavens there were this transformation to the calm master and the dutiful peon. She stares at him, opens her dark grayish eyes and said, "You wanted us to say, 'Dawg!'" Shadows recollected her looking intently at him as if she wanted to slap him. In this case behavioral protocol or common sense dictates she leave first, or tell him to leave, or if he was fast enough he could just run. But she had chased him and caught him sometime ago… Eventually she turns around and strides away muttering. She was smiling too. She likes his joke…and he escaped too.

Now it seems like it was so long ago in time, but the family emotions are still active…

CHAPTER 3

MISCELLANEOUS SOCIAL RESPONSES

People in his old Villages were always talking about pickpockets and thieves in the towns, or how hungry and devious town folks were. "*Dem a ginnal— con artistes!*" was the usual outcry. In other words a *town man* was a city "*ginnal*" that is always ready to play the Brer Anancy tricks on you, so always be on your guard with them. It should be noted that "town man" also meant the "town woman." They don't care about the gender; they were all *ginals*. If you should leave the country and return to visit, your friends and family would greet you with the joke, "So you turn a *town ginal* now." The town women were considered too pretty, too clean and too dressed-up to be of any use. This was the vocal male sentiment before their countrywomen until it gets dark…! Country folks are always returning from the city to praises from their neighbors that they are safe. They would tell tales of how they outsmarted the city pickpockets and were not robbed. Years later Shadows finally got to meet one of these town robbers near what the sellers called the "Grass Yard," at the corner of Darling Street and Spanish Town Road in Kingston. He picked Shadows businessman uncle, "The Pharaoh." That thief made a dangerous mistake! As the guys in the town would respectfully say, "The Pharaoh doesn't romp!" He chased the thief across the streets with his knife cutting at the thief's flying shirt. The striding fellow looked back at the sharp glistening blade coming down over his shoulder. He quickly tossed the stolen wallet towards his "confederate," and instantly finds a higher speed to save his life. His uncle hastily changed direction towards his "flying" wallet. He grabbed it out of mid air before the fumbling "confederate" and a couple of their noisy gang members could react. The sweating and angry "Pharaoh!" just stood there in a belligerent mood with a wicked looking shoemaker knife in his right hand, daring any of them to show a willingness to fight. He then made eye contact with the nearest thief, stiffened his right hand with the sharp glistening blade, slowly walked towards him and hissed, "Mi nuh in a no long argument!" The guy quailed. The thieving group made threats from a safe distance and then cautiously backed away. The country passengers on the bus made no effort to help; they were just too frightened to get involved. When Shadows tried going outside to help his uncle the alarmed passengers shouted: "sit down!" He nervously sat and watched. But now he still wonders if that was sound advice, seeing that no adult were willing to lend his uncle a helping hand. In those days there were no mercy shown to thieves…except by the police.

He remembers his mother taking him to "town." Everyone from the country parts was always yearning to go to *town*. He recalls seeing the Hydro-Electric Station, at Kent Village where those men lost their lives in 1904… When his parents tell him the tale he believed that it had happened recently. Perhaps they remembered names and events like the African village *griots*— mental record keeper. It should be remembered that the older folks never tell you about numeric dates. The older folks like his grandmother is always using historical milestones as, "In Missis Queen days such and such occurs…or could not happen." The Missis Queen is the British monarch, Queen Victoria. As a child Shadows always think about those poor men drowning in an enclosed place… That was such a scary tale. It was scarier than sleeping in a darkened, supposedly "haunted" house in Maggotty, and expecting something awful to happen, then drifted off to sleep and awake in the morning; being glad you survived the ordeal, but still wondering what happened during your sleeping time. In later life he understood how industrial accidents occur especially without proper communication and very poor supervisions.

It was also on this road that he demystified the traveling of the mysterious fisherman. Over the last year in school, Shadows pondered where the "whistle blowing" fisherman comes from? Now he meets him; hustling along the paved road, in the gorge. This time he was not blowing his whistle. That fisherman was always coming from the Bog Walk road, passing his school; riding a bicycle with an iced box of fishes behind him on a carrier. He would notify his customers by occasionally blowing his whistle and shouts, "Fresh fish!" Shadows young mind then could not even imagine where the sea was. This man would ride his bicycle many miles from the sea to the hinterland villages and small hamlets on rough stony roads. Then there were always his customer's questions, "Is your fish fresh?" But of course he would always say yes. I know, this begs the question where a *fisherman never says his fish is otherwise*.

At that time no one was available to tell how electricity was generated. His mother got the information through his father. He now wonders if his ingenious brother then knew how? The Bog Walk gorge was like a Cosmic Revelation with it was coolness, beautiful landscape and daunting high embankments. Then there was Flat Bridge, a name that conjures up all type of frightening emotions for travelers. Shadows, his mother and their friends stopped at the bridge. He went up in the hills to pick mangoes and naseberries with a boyhood school friend. The most competent, bareback, "horse riding" person he has ever seen. Those guys playing Indians in the Western movies were like child's play to his young friend. Shadows went into the water almost under the bridge and there goes all the Flat Bridge mysteries... At that time he could not swim. And that was years before he almost drowned after school at the place called "Lawn," below the dam, a couple of miles away. As he tried touching the bridge, his mother sat there looking at him. She surprises him by not commanding that he should come out of the water. She was silent but watchful. He knew even now that he had reached his limitation when he nearly touched the concrete structure. He heard her voice without her vocally calling him. He retreated and returned ashore. She was quiet and her jaw was taut. She was staring into space as if averting her eyes. She was probably scared and angry because he had pushed her to the limit in front of strangers. They became very quiet for the rest of the trip...He was too happy to be of concern. He was going to town, and he was on the outskirts too. That is where all his families were. On reaching *town*

Shadows bade farewell to his last boyhood friend from his rural school. He had never again seen the friendly and ingenious bareback *horse rider.* Such is the life of a child. That phase of his rural life ended with that simple departure. We made friends and loss them at the whims of our families transitions. A few years later when he almost drowned at Lawn she was incense and vocally warned him if he ventures on living dangerously she would just tie a piece of white calico around her waist, weep, ripped it in two, and then buried him with one half. He had a vague idea that the ripped calico symbolizes an ultimate separation between family members...a tragic loss but life goes on! He then wondered how she heard about the incident. A friend enlightened him that her *favorite niece*, his friendly cousin did the honor. Shadows at that time had the common sense to let sleeping dogs lie as he continues his quest for better swimming techniques. As Shadows compile thoughts; he reviews former visions of the old, noisy and historic town, and concluded that few positive changes have occurred here. It is now dirty, congested and noisy...as his mother and her generations always said it was, but he also remembers the enjoyable nocturnal pursuits he had here.

It was indeed a pleasant place in times gone by. Now here they use rough police tactics to clear peddlers from their rickety, smelly and overcrowded sidewalks. There is not much cooperation here between the citizen and the police. Shadows looked at the old peaceful town's decaying infrastructure and felt a slight pang of disgust. The once quiet sidewalks were uneven, cracked, and dirty and transformed into a

Mecca for rowdy street vendors. The once orderly public transportation system was non-existence. He now romanticized about his old town, but even then it was dilapidated, but it was home and practically crime free. There is no tennis being played here, anyway that was for the upper and middle class. The distinction of dressing in white sent the image that there was a different level of social acceptance and of course there was. Cricket was a bit different; it was a mass movement game. This is a cricket town where champions reside. It was said that the West Indies started Test cricket in 1928 so there is a high level of cricket playing here. Tennis was a Country Club event that deals with the color white for both skins and clothing, except for the black skinned ball boys ... Inertia has prevails here.

THE AUTOMAN

It was on the outskirts of this decaying town that Shadows spent most of his adolescent life. His friends lived here then. It is still in this town that his true family roots are now sustained (planted)... It was here that he spent the latter part of his childhood and his adolescent years. They were good and bad times too, but most were very good times. Shadows trek through life in the company of family stalwarts and friends. These people were not publicized; neither do they have accolades or quickly remembered names on the human social rosters; but they were always there when he needed them. People like the Automan, the last of the family's urban pioneers. A confidante likes a father figure. He showed Shadows the ecstasy of sport, the information in the library, and the cinema…and paid his way for his education, and also the security of a good home. He was the building block for a good life. He vividly remembers the Automan's scary story about a burning commercial building across the street from him. His girlfriend awoke him during the fire. He became disoriented and frightened by the intense heat and commotion outside. The house was made of board, a real attraction for sparks! He just could not remember where the doorway was. He kept jumping on the walls in his vain attempts to exit the room. His girlfriend restrained him and they escaped. The Automan always remembers her in good grace for that single incident. At that time he had no idea the fire was next door. Shadows recollected that in all these fires, if the slow running fire brigade arrives on time to save the day, there is generally no water in the main. Sometime Shadows wonders why they even have this service. But that is unfair to the firemen, because Shadows observed these same firemen working feverishly against all those odds to save a neighbor's home.

Shadows reminisces on a few childhood skirmishes and misadventures with the Automan. His favorite misadventure was seeing the movies from a tree. The tree was in someone's home in one of these upscale areas. They were separated in different trees. It appears the Automan was told to leave and he left without Shadows. The nervous male servant came with a kindly Caucasian woman, his employer who gracefully asks Shadows to leave… In looking back on that incident it appears that the Automan's friend lost his job. Again his mother heard about the incident from

29

another woman. What is it with the woman's network? Then there was the bicycle accident and the pain... The Automan refused commenting that he sent Shadows on an errand. Perhaps that would have given some merit to his being on the street. It was here that the Auntie decided to spank instead of applying some healing... It was a slight touch, but he noticed his mother said nothing. Shadows always keep away from his Auntie after that, especially when he realized that his mom did not reprimand her. He knew his mom did not like it, because he saw her face. They only know to afflict physical pain...isn't the accident painful enough. With all the childhood pain, the Automan and he are always on the same side where sports are concern...they are in truth kindred souls walking on a Spiritual journey... He remembers his first ride on a bicycle's carrier. He was so proud to have a family riding a bicycle at such fast speed. His friends he knew were very envious. He had never before been made to feel outstanding among his friends. This time he was really enjoying it...Now it seems so trivial, but then among the rural villages it was a special treat, speeding at break neck speed on a new bicycle! We did not ask for much then...perhaps we just did not know how. He also remembers his first bicycle solo ride. This was another uncle too, who gave him the freedom to ride, and also the interesting treat of sampling the cool mixture of malted milk with porter while in town. His uncles from his mother's side were great guys to him. He knew he did nothing special to inherit their loving treatment; it was a gift from their sister who was always considerate towards them... "Cast your bread upon the water..." He is not in anyway faulting the only uncle from the other side, for they say, "Whom the gods love die young."

Shadows recalls the town dwellers rising during the early mornings of the cane season; talking in hushed tones in their homes, and on the streets while preparing food and transportation for work. He finally paid a visit to one of these plantations, to the Innswood Sugar Estates. Some of the workers spoke about a property ranger called Rhygin. At that time there was a difference between a ranger, a headman and a *busha*. He had problem understanding the difference between a headman and a busha. The guy "Rhygin" was another of the big, bad and rough Black men used to control other Blacks. (It should be noted that the word *rhygin* has a special significance in the culture; not necessarily bad either. So be as *rhygin* as you choose to be.) His role was to enforce discipline with brute force. "The mentality was using force but never to teach respect for another Black person." Shadows believed he had observed a slice of what the slave plantation must have been. Today, we still see this level of disrespect among the children of our fore parents who refer to each other as "streggeh" gals and "hurry cum up" boys, while kowtowing to people of whiter shades as Mister and Missis. Is this where an American once said, "Grab their mind early and their unaware ass will follow…" No White or Chinese were seen cutting canes. There were rumors of inhumane treatment meted out by the ranger to those who stole mangoes. Apparently the law was more for property protection and not for people's rights. Ripe Bombay mangoes were everywhere, untouched. Things were orderly. They called the general manager a Pharaoh.

He was a strong disciplinarian and a keen sportsman. He was Black, and that was a great surprise. In this cane cutting era workers would credit food then hide during payday when the bill is due. Shadows heard of an incident when a hungry *one-eyed* worker "trusts" (credits) food from a woman until payday. When the lady tries to collect she could not find *this* one-eyed man. Remember, during those times most persons would only give you a first name, or some nickname. Just don't ask for their full name or they would get outrageously angry and suspicious that you were prying. If you are unarmed (or armed) it is very foolish to get a cane cutter with a *bill* (the cane cutting tool) angry! Anyway, she asked another man if he knew the *one-eyed* man working here, he told her no. She was actually asking the conniving man who has now opened both his eyes. The place was overrun with non-cane cutting gamblers during paydays. They enticed these compulsive and foolish cane cutters to play cards and dice games in the "interval"— the paths between cane fields. In other words they psychologically ambushed them on the tracts on their way home... "I have 30 pounds with me; here it is. Don't you want to win back some of your money?" The gambler probably has some pretty young woman sitting in a lewd fashion with all these bills in front of her. She is a plant to entice him...

Shadows now reflects on those daily interplay between men and women, and the misguided thinking that the grass is greener on the other side... In those days many women were not being employed outside of their homes. If they were ever employed, it was always at a lower rate than men. During the cane season women generally were used for *loading* canes on trucks. They were generally never cane cutters. A couple male cane cutters told Shadows that they were not too keen on women cutters. It seems they met a couple female cutters that were just too good. The men had problems keeping up with them. We can understand the dilemma here...in a *rough and tumble world* you are having the physically weaker gender, the female *out rough and tumbling* the male! This could never be good gender politics in a bigoted patriarchal world. The class division in the society was indelible...so was the gender bias. There were always people trying to make a big economic score during the cane crop. During this season most men are looking for the prettiest and most outstanding women they can get: "*mi nuh want no chu galang gal*" –unschooled gal! Because they now have money, and are therefore a force to be reckoned with. The women on the other hand are out to get the man (or men) with the most earning, thereby excusing appearance with: "*if him a even Brother Anancy mi can give him some fancy!*" At this time "looks" goes out of the windows because money talks. Even as a young child Shadows looked at the cane field workers, and realized that their level of hardship was extreme. It was much more tedious than sawing boards with a big-rip saw as was done by Mass Thaddy and his son Cecil did that early morning among the cool cocoa and mango plants in the gully. At least they had big "*sawer-man's dumplings*"—huge flour dumplings. Board sawing was the only form of work he had witnessed other than the usual field cultivations. The cane field was hot, sticky and outright hellish. Although the factory machinery and the tractors fascinated him, he then made a mental note that such work was not for him. Years later he found out that this same cane cultivation he so heavily despised was the main cause of the forced Black migration from across the seas… "It must be the spirits of his ancestors calling out for his avoidance!"

At the top of the cane field labor hierarchy is the high paid Tractor driver. Every woman has her eyes on him. Shadows recollected a tractor driver who came home to a barren house because his deceiving sweetheart had removed his furniture to some unknown location in the country. The poor misguided fellow was so used to his bed always behind his bedroom door. He usually just threw his weary body on the bed. Alas! This time there was no bed. He dropped on his back and passed out. His pretty sweetheart was missing. He had to be nourished back to health by his former older woman next door that he now vows never to leave again…after he finds his furniture in the country. Furniture recovery was never easy because the thieves are always having names like Sweety, Jeany, Nicey, Gladys, Lovey or some outlandish pronunciations ending with the letter wye. But why is this so? Is there a comforting male reaction in connection with female names ending with the letter "y?" One wonders what special gift women represent with names ending in wyes. These cutters must have known of a hidden solace with a "y-word" ending! And these women are always from the "country" parts. And here again is another male preference for a wye ending word. The psychology here is that country people are supposed to be mentally slow, but very honest; so the reasoning is that most men would be happier getting a docile country lass. Alas! That is where they made the mistake. These women never come from any specific parish. How about, "I am from down the country!" Never a specific parish… If a man should ask, "What is your name?" "Call mi Sweety…" Never any surname… They were all versed in the art of the one-named chicanery play. And they were not even single-named ace Brazilian football players…Just don't ask them they will tell you they are! Then there were those guys who were *cane cutters* and wanted to get the tractor driver's respect. One cane cutter did not wish his new woman to know he was not a tractor driver. He confused her by saying he drives the *engine bill*. She surprised him with lunch one day. His friends pointed him out as over there cutting cane, or "*raising cane,*" as they would say then. She asked him why he lied. He replied, "I said the *engine bill*. I did not say a tractor. You want a tractor driver…?" They smile in understanding, and moved along with their lives. Pride and a desire for social acceptance make us do many strange things. It is the same reason for a wife having a refrigerator full of food while her husband and children are dying of hunger. Or having furniture your family cannot sit on; it's just for showing off. This is the behavior of the status climbing upper St. Andrew types in those days where even the maids were pulling off styles that they did not want any "*hurry-cum-up*" – uncouth boy. To counterbalance this feminine reaction the yard-boys are always announcing they did not want any "*streggeh gal.*" –insipid and low class. It seems such was the new class division between the latter day house and field hands of former slaves. The maids' big score was trying to out-dress their employer's wife.

Doing that always leads to certain trouble; not "love in the house!" They were so Victorian with pretenses. People then were always using the *Upper St. Andrew* labels as a yardstick for social standards. To eat a large meal was considered uncouth and low class. You were required to eat small quantities as the British white ruling groups were supposed to be doing. Many of the ordinary people had never seen these people at meal, but the numerous maids relayed this information to the working class. In the case of the deep desire to acquire furniture, that type of behavior seems to persist with immigrants who still see owning new furniture or a car as a more valuable asset than buying a house or taking care of their children's future.

Shadows is reminded of other gender politics and the resulting economical problems arising from the miscalculations of sexual control. His primary lesson on inter-personal relationships was an incidence he usually refers to as the *feminist crossing triad*. He remembers how two women of a feminist double crossing *triad* played a losing game. The feminist triad consisted of two younger brown-skinned women and an older dark-skinned one. One of the younger women works. The older lady, and the other, the prettiest of the triad did not. The group usually meets in seclusion at the older woman's house. The older woman knew the economic danger that lurks in the social shadows for any non-professional and uneducated female loser with children in this two-timing game called "*giving bun*" –infidelity. Anyway, she coaxed her working friend in helping her "sweet boy" —cool brother— migrates to England. This was more than economic help. The agreement was first to help her brother with cash. He would then return it to help others. Unfortunately these were mere promises. When the deal became sour the older woman did everything to deny her involvement and remains with her husband. She knew where her bread was buttered. The other two women were thrown to the wolves as *two-timers.* The prettiest woman husband left her. The prettiest woman was always beautifully dressed; had never worked before, and did not know how to compete in the workplace. Her life was completely wrecked. She eventually went insane. The other younger woman was a shadow of her former self after her man from childhood got wind of her plan. The man observed the new changing realities and walked out to find a new social approach. He found an older more socially versatile mate. He then decided to get married. The deceptive older friend's brother abandoned the working female at this time, so she decided to make one last stand to reclaim her lover. In desperation she went to her ex-lover's fiancé's job and caused a fuss. Shadows recollects how surprise and sorrowful he was at this turn of affairs. But then he compared the vibrancy of the present wife with that of the former mate. He met the former mate many years later and still see the haunting stare in her eyes after all these years... The unfortunate thing is the husband's families; especially the females have this unbounded preference for her over all these years. This incident had warned Shadows that sometimes families can be so far out of sync with reality.

CHAPTER 4

DEMPSHIRE PEN

He remembers his uncle's first home as a place of joy and happiness. It was not in one of those upscale neighborhoods people like to fantasize about, but it was home. At this time he can only laugh at the builder, a cobbler-like carpenter who made so many mistakes. We were all happy there with his young children and other extended family from the country parts, along with his special dog, "Spot." Spot was treated as a true family member. She was definitely no little playful Joslyn! Her intimidation and ferocity were programmed with silence…. She once grabbed the neighbor's bag and caused a lawsuit… After that incident, the poor man was afraid to come home. Shadows recollected trying his hand at bedtime story telling to a young girl. His made-up tale was about some horse riding Arabian character called Sir Hokey Dokes. It frightening the poor child so much she had vicious nightmares. The surprising part is the following nights she again asks for the same story. When he tried deviating a little from the previous night's scary script she would have none of that; she wanted the original gory story intact! She would soon drop off to sleep and he would be left in the dark a little scared. He had never liked that frightful story. The original tale usually gave him the chills. To him then it was a bit too weird. Shadows remembered he had to be firm about not telling that tale again. When he tried replacing it, she was never satisfied with another made up tale. When he tried his new tale of "Habbleza Hulleza the Arabian story teller" she was mildly satisfied. He finally nicknamed her "Habbleza Hulleza" because her older relatives blamed her for carrying news to her mom about their conduct. His unnerving story telling was long ago before he knew about Halloween and the numerous scary and ghoulish Hollywood entertainment markets. Remember during this time books were scarce and at a premium. Stories like Santa Claus were just a mere whisper.

Santa was like a flying *red dressed demon* that trespassed in your home at the dead of night, at precisely twelve midnight, when you are asleep, and when only the most *dangerous ghosts and destructive rolling calves* with chains inhabited the dark *outsides*. Get these details correctly; pay attention, if you can inculcate the young with this idea then you have no need stuffing Christmas presents in a sack, then all Queen Victoria husband's accredited effort of introducing the Klaus Guy to the Empire will possibly fade away (after he empties his bags of goodies.) The pulling *female reindeers* could then reign supreme in their Arctic homeland... Merchants beware, take a stand now! Tehehehe...

There were so many adolescent pranks; unfortunately some eventually results in adult responsibility....OOPS! He remembers his in-law being caught in his own room with the neighbor's daughter. The poor confused girl fled through a window trying to deflect the scandal... The man sequestered himself for days in his room, being afraid of facing the outside world. Many people denied scandals until there is that typical "showing" and the question, "Girl whose baby is it?" Then the puss is out of the bag and there will be no more childish play ground taunting of, "Tell, tell, tell till your belly swell!" Shadows himself was almost caught in the neighbor's house. That was an embarrassing incident where he lost a shirt button in the process. The lady's brother playing the super detective rushed out on the street asking who was in his house. The guy was brilliant. He even tried matching the button on Shadow's shirt... Shadows used sophistry to deflect his guilt. The smart brother seems to believe the story. But then the brother is smart... There were always some special nightly episodes. On one of these occasions Shadows mistakenly went to the wrong house! Apparently he did not pay much attention to the house where the girl went. There was a house in the direction she pointed, but her house was behind the first house. Details! Details...? Alas! Shadows went to the house in front. It was dark the way he likes it, so he softly knocks on the door. A man opened the door. The dim light in the room showed his green striped underwear. He stretched, rakishly scratched his belly and then yawned outrageously, shook his head and loudly bellowed, "*A weh di r... you want now!*" He yawned again, and Shadows disappeared... That alarming voice was the constantly cussing and threatening voice from the hilltop! In the man's rage Shadows preferred giving no truthful explanation, so he ran to cover up his mistakes and thereby conceals his identity. This was the hostile neighbor's house that is always creating a disturbance. That man was continually threatening to destroy any man who tries *fooling* with his woman. While on his swift journey Shadows could hear him broadcasting to the neighborhood, telling them that his woman "*a keep man with him.*" The lesson learnt there was to be very specific with directions whenever you are going on any business. Beware, don't be jumpy and time-shifted ahead to what you are going to do later; get the correct information first, and then be able to use it wisely…!

WILY MIGRATIONS (50s/60s)

Talking about going in a specific direction, the British migration period was rife with *fare departure intrigues.* Everyone was trying to see a way to get his or her fares to England. "Mi ah gaa a England!"—I am going to England, was the dominant speech those days. Now everyone was your friend…and your social acceptance had just jumped numerous notches. You would become quite popular because people believe you could do something for them. That "something" was to take them *up there* with you, or make contact for them in England. The "u*p there"* always means England. "Mi hear say you ah go up?" was not a question about the paradise of Heaven. It was one asking if you are migrating to England, viewed then as the economical haven. The general transportation mode was first by ships for about 75 pounds. It took about 3 weeks then. Later transportation was by planes and then non-stop flight for 3 days costing about 85 or 100 Pounds. Those who could afford the quick plane trips were considered a better class. People really did like social classes in those days… If you want to hide out from the law or the irate "*baby mother*" types, or from some hostile or jealous male, or a destructive female; just circulate rumors that you "gone a England!" Going to the US then was not a priority unless you were mildly insane. People then associate Jim Crow with John Crow. England was the place to be. The desire for going to Canada was far below a whisper...

With this hawkish migration desires, arises a series of connivances among departing immigrants. The wife of one of Shadows' town neighbors rented a room to a tenant. A few

weeks later, the tenant gave his notice to leave. Everyone knew he was going to England so that was no big thing. The following morning the wife asked a friend to "give an eye" (watch) on her two children. The hours passed into evening and she did not return. Finally the husband came from work. He had a few beers and waited. His older son by a former marriage eventually told him that he suspected that she will not return. It came out that the tenant was the wife's former school lover from the country...we are in the town and country seesaw, one more time. They had made a pact to leave for England that morning.

In those days people did whatever contrivances it took to get away from the island. Some were coping the best ways they could. For others the end justifies the means. Some would steal from people on the island, by not returning the money so others could migrate, or by not going to the person in England who sent for them. Then there was the young country man sitting outside in the darkness smoking a ganja *spliff* and using a "muttering strategy" to verbally threaten his parents over his England fare. He acted as if he was out there alone in the darkness enjoying his smokes and muttering to himself what he will have to do next day if he has to again asked for some parental help. "A me a do all the work and the old gal dem all gone away. If this continue me have fi just bevel me machete and do wey mi have fi do…a hoe!" His sisters who had never put much effort into the family livestock were sent away with much fanfare…usually the entire district doing a mass movement by accompanying the lonely migrant to the ship. Now you can understand the camaraderie of a country village! A boy was never adored in this family; he was the raggedy unschooled *cinde*-fellow type who does the entire dirty pastoral and manual works in the home. (This was not an uncommon social behavior for many families. The girls were the little princesses and the boys were the little field hands.) When the parents settled in their bed and heard his rambling outside they decided he was just too dangerous to have around anymore. The next day he got his fare to England. Unfortunately others were not so lucky… They had *to suck salt through wooden spoons* – bear massive hardships to get their fares. Some even had to drop out of society and live in huts in the woods to raise the necessary money for their England fares. Others raise livestock and even "borrowed" some of their parent's livestock during the nights to make up their fares.

CHAPTER 5

BUFF — "SOCIAL REALITIES ON THE STREETS"

At this time there were others who had no desire, made no effort, or have no resources to go to England. For these guys in the towns, the streets were their hustling scenes. Remember, this was during the days when the British hanged people and cart the bodies for burial at Tawes Pen...the black horse-drawn hearse being unceremoniously driven through the town by a man dressed in a black gown. Many young people then had problem believing the social images. Perhaps the British were using subtle images to confront another Mau Mau problem. The society had radically changed after the 1951 hurricane. After that emergency, *tent dwellers* were placed in permanent homes, or Homestead. Shadows observed that Nature destroys the thin social fabric of the society resulting in what is known as *ghettoization* of the struggling urban dwellers. There was an eroding of the social order with this mixing of people in close proximity. This natural disaster wreaked havoc with the discipline as the schools were closed for a long period of time after the hurricane.

Anyway, guys in the urban areas are so different from rural folks. In his youth Shadows liked living in the city, it was fun although the country-style living still stays within his soul. Now it finally manifests itself as a command to his better way of life. He remembers the shenanigans of the irascible and streetwise Buff. Buff was one of these guys from a smaller country town. The general economic state has people moving from the rural to the urban areas in search of better living. Buff was an adolescent when he ended at Shadows uncle's business. He learned a trade and then become a salesman. He did well at that too. On one of his salesman escapade he mentions how he "*late*" the other competing merchants. The term "late" was the in-word then, meaning to beats the competition. Shadows recollects his meeting Buff for the first time. Buff had just returned from his first sales trip. He was about five-eleven, 180 pounds of well-developed body. He leaned against the wooden door patting his well cosmetic hairdo with his right hand. His left was in his belt as if he was about to draw his six-gun in some old B-rate movie. Shadows knew later that all this was a studied pose to reflect the tough guy's image from the various movies. His shirt was half opened showing his pecks. He has to let everyone know that he lifts weights. On recollection now his hair resembles the hairstyle worn by the singer Little Richard of the "Long Tall Sally" rock and roll fame. Buff too had the dark skin type. He was well fed, exuding the cocksure attitude of youthfulness as if saying, "Look at me...I am the Buff!" He was just smiling while calmly dramatizing his stories. It seems he met a virgin that had three children...really. It seems that Buff found her story contrary after they had a *sales affair*.

Buff likes the movies. To him it was not like a make believe, it was more like reality right there on the silver screen. And it better be an action movie. To the guys on the streets, movie stars were real heroes…that is worthy of long debates. Shadows still remembers the "Thunder before lightening" debate. It was so hard to get Buff and his cronies to accept that lightening comes before thunder! They choose to believe the "thunder before lightening" approach. Don't try convincing some of these guys otherwise. Anyway, they will eventually come back later and tell you they were just testing you. All smiles and everyone was again happy. Then they would spend a couple days laughing at each other for believing the wrong thing. There would be numerous "But a test mi a test you. Mi want fi see how far you a go tek that type of foolishness…" How about science is Obeah? That was a super sensitive topic with an unspoken question of *because you go further than me in school; you think you can fool me?* This is where good friends back down and laugh it off. Buff had a calm spirited coworker named Hook Arrow. They both had their eyes on the same young fair skinned damsel. It seems that The Hook and Buff concocted up a plan to "mouth" or *utter a few lyrics to the daughta* one night. The defined mission of the plan was to help The Hook; unfortunately it appears Buff had his own designs. As usual Buff primped up his buff hair style and ripped off a few melodies on his Harmonica "mouth organ" to the delight of the young lady. "The Hook" by then stuttered and lost his *speech*…and had to endure weeks of ribbing from his competitor calling him an Admiral *bent bow*. Buff believes he was a good "mouth organ" player; he was really good too. He was encouraged to go on one of the local Monday nights "Talent Parade" shows. He likes singing like Louis 'Satchmo'

Armstrong in his gravely voice but he never did enter. This was indeed a very good decision. We could just imagine Buff and his friends believe he won the contest and the judges think otherwise! Those Talent Parades were the most rowdy places to be. Many of the Ska, rock steady and reggae artistes came from these talent scenes. These artistes are the survivors of the most abusive crowds imaginable. Things were even thrown at these poor artistes while they were being vocally abused.

Buff has numerous stories; especially those touching on some amorous relationships and of course the movies. (Whenever Buff tells a story, or *"stars"* in one of his make-up movies you should listen and laugh too. He likes that. No, he was not Stalin, but he could be a very good friend...) His famous story was his taking a *piece* in the old cemetery. He claimed the ghost stood nearby waiting: no not to get *some*, but to get home, down into the tomb. The ghost *cut his eyes* at them when his woman lay prone on the tomb, she hugged him and whispered that they were not going to give that ugly man standing there any. She then fainted when they got up and the ghost nonchalantly slides down inside the tomb... Why these people have this impression that ghostly spirits must be hideous? Were these guys reading Dickens', "A Christmas Carol?" If ghosts or *duppies are so* ugly or undesirable, then why are people always dreaming of these unsightly spirits? Perhaps the *duppies* are the one in control!

Because of his great love of the movies Buff became trendy. He copied the in vogue movie star Tony Curtis' looks onto a Black face. The hairstyle was called the *buff*. Actually no one knew Buff's real

47

name. No one really wanted to ask either. He said his name was Buff, so be it…What was his age? Well, he was always in his teens until some one of the respected "mentor" types mentioned, "The way you were behaving last year I thought you were 18." He grumbled that he was going into his nineteen. No, he was not Peter Pan; neither had he heard of the guy. But he was a young man in his teen. Buff was irascible but kind, industrious and straight laced honest! Shadows witnessed Buff's first fight with *Strangler* Wright, the neighborhood rum head. Then there was the blowout episode with his good friend *Big Dog Roy (BDR)*…These two guys would invite each other during the evening, "You going to '*sit down' tonight*?" meaning are you going to the movies. There were many double and triple bill showings. After the first movie, the wily BDR was always leaving; telling Buff there is a girl over the other section he wanted to take home with him. One night Buff left early because the actions were not to his liking, "*de star boy was too soft and lovey-dove wid de ole double crossing star gal…*" Remember that Buff takes his movies very seriously; it was a piece of real life! When he reached home his girlfriend, Zunny ran from the house down the dark path screaming, "Murder!" He hardly paid her mind when he fleetingly asks what is wrong with her. He then cautiously took out his sharp pearl handle dagger from his scabbard (like any star boy), and flexed his muscles. He noticed his bed was not firmly on the floor and there were bare feet hanging out. He used the side of his dagger and drew it across the foot bottom, shouting, "Come out…!" BDR emerges! Buff calmly said, "Man me never know it was you; if me know it was you mi would make you enjoy yourself!" Hook Arrow first broke the news because he was BDR's friend. Shadows can still see Buff's face while telling him the story the next day. He was calm and jovial. It seems he was more concern that BDR, one of the "toughest" looks very silly hiding under a very low bed. Zunny tried hiding out forever. This was the same woman who threatened Buff and his lover in a dark room with a broken bottle. She then brought the quiet street into wakefulness that night by again crying, "Murder, dem kill Buff!" At this time Buff was considered a peanut capitalist with whistling peanut pushed carts that he hired out. He always has cash so the women on the streets adored him. He finally found Zunny. A youthful Shadows then pleaded with him not to hurt her. He agreed, but promised teaching her a lesson by spanking her with his "*willow*!" That was a strange saying because Buff of course was no cricketer, and he had no visible bat. He decided on evenly sharing everything with her, including his bed. To prove he was serious he brought his new girlfriend home to share his *front* part of the bed and gave Zunny the back nearest to the wall! I hope everyone understands by now why Buff did not give her the front of the bed! Buff decided on searching for another lover because Zunny was unfaithful, and returning to her would cause him to lose face with his friends. In those society you cannot act as if you are jealous, because that would make you appears as "too soft." Then, that was very bad when someone accused you as being "led away by women." With this cultural concept in mind, Buff one night went searching for a new love. Apparently he told his new, young idol worshipping, peeping tom apprentice friend; the altar boy turned *street denizen, Knotty Goat Head.* The "Head" tried trailing the couple in the dark to the rendezvous. The slick and streetwise proposed "replacement" sense that they were being followed. She informed Buff that they should set a trap, and he should keep on talking and walking in the dark and she will take care of the intruder. The trick worked. She eventually *"bricked"* down the unsuspecting Head and walked away to their rendezvous where she gave him a *short sample*. He agreed the sample was good so she request a donation to complete the transaction. Being the Buff, *you do not pay for play*. It should be the other way around… This time he decides on making an exception. He found himself short of cash and tried a little trickery. In the darkness the play unraveled when the woman felt the edges of each coin to determine their worth. It appears few half-crowns and a few shillings and sixpences were not enough! She tossed the money away in the darkness, then chided Buff for being unfair to a friend and someone who always freely "soothes his pains." The next day a chastened Buff admitted he lost a friend through greed. Apparently his ineffective search and odd sleeping arrangements did not work too well because he finally forgave Zunny.

Shadows finally saw Buff tactfully backs down when he foolishly challenged a dangerous man named "Panty" who sneered at him that if he is such a tough man, then Buff needs no dagger to fight him. The end of the Buff's saga came when he tangled with the secretive, but super cool workman name Tony, and was brutally knifed. Tony did surprises everyone with his "numerous vacations," but he really tried avoiding that conflict. Buff's final neighborhood error came when he roughed up Zunny and caused her severe pain. This resulted in Zunny's spiritual separation from Buff. He was repentant, and very sad. As a final separation act the Pharaoh banished him from his business sites. He left home and strikes out on his own. This for Shadows was the end of an era. We later all grew up and moved towards different parts of the society. Buffy was eventually diagnosed with a mental problem, certified madness. He went through a few pain and sufferings but eventually re-emerged as a city capitalist and later changed his direction to the country hills. He then played with politics and business in a changing world...the former was definitely not his forte.

The last time Shadows spoke with him, it was a changed and more mature Buff. He finally gave up his Hollywood-like "buff" hairstyle; denigrating it as "*a Babylonian dress code unworthy of a Blackman.*" He finally sees himself not as a supporter for Hollywood styles or clothing but as an individual... We were then viewing things from a different perspective, although Buff had still asked if Shadows was going to the movies later—"*you ah go sit down*?" Shadows replied no, and reflected on their younger days, during the vivacious "Buff-time" when Buff had a tendency of *parading* without shirts...a shirtless body frightens people. It reminds them of the threat of wild and "uncivilized" ungodly un-Christian like African primitives...a state they wholeheartedly tried to forget with a great deal of European persuasion! Shadows remembered his Auntie got very outrageous because

Buff *towed* her daughter on a bicycle. His uncle, the Pharaoh warns Buff against such actions... It was more like a stern rebuke to keep away from our family. "We are all friendly here but we recognized your threat!"

Actually there is nothing wrong with being clothed, or perhaps being naked. It depends on the society you are in. Shadows has a friend who stumbled on a nudist camp, and was so ashamed because he was the only one wearing clothes. He fled to the nearest shelter. On the other side Shadows remembered two police detectives tried arresting a ganja smoker in an old cemetery. The man fought their efforts by removing his clothes. They tried putting his clothes on before arresting him. The smoker resisted until the police eventually gave up and he escaped. Culturally people believe nakedness should not be shown in public. We are not actually in Southern Sudan in the 20th Century. Nakedness is a deterrent, but that cannot be said for the two naked men who raided the yam market at Alley during the height of the 1951 hurricane. First it was believed that they were keeping their clothes dry someplace else, but when the women were exhorted to apprehend them, all the aggressive "higglers" refused saying they were not going to apprehend some naked "*long tone man*!" Is there something sinister, funny or screwy with the idea of a clothed woman apprehending a naked man in the darkness? The women were just contented to make faces at them from the shelter of the market house...they actually acted as if they did not see them!

CHAPTER 6

SEX AND RIBALDRY

Shadows recalled his first test on how to handle questions of amorous relationships between a man and his woman. The question came from his recent Country friend from Portland, "West the Aggressor," while working at the Post Office. His friend told him that he visited his new City-girlfriend, and she has a man covered up with a white sheet on her bed. He asked her who the man was. She replied she did not know. The Aggressor asked Shadows opinion. Shadows diplomatically retorted the man could have lost his way… The "Aggressor" curiously eyeballed him then calmly walked away as if in deep thoughts. Later he returned a bit more animated, exclaiming, "That is foolishness. She must know him." By this time Shadows was in his late teens and could not be easily trifled with in this manner… The Aggressor was his first beer-drinking buddy after work…one very cool guy too.

It brings up the point. When do young ones know you have *"finally arrived"* at maturity. Is it whenever an older respectful family member or relatives openly referred to sexual subjects without being embarrassed? A time when euphemism is being left behind! "Look at the little *piss-pot weak-back* bull calf. Not even have any use." Shadows reminisces his irate Auntie pointing to a troublesome bull calf as an example of the male's incompetence to satisfy a lover? "Asking for *something* you can't manage..." Now, when a highly respected matriarchal family member openly addressed you with such words then you know you are moving into aged respectability, or in the *"big-people's"* group. He recalls nervously adjusted his face muscles in a laughing mask. He was surprised with this level of conversation from an always respectful, noisily praying and Bible reading Auntie. Some of her other couched sensual grumblings also came to mind, "Sake a some of you mi cannot even say mi prayers in peace a night! Onoo no bother me...come out a mi yard!" This couched request to leave home took him quite a few years to unravel. One of his female cousins finally enlightened him on that one. It seems she had used too much vocal energy in her *dance of life...*

A favorite jaunt for boys and girls were a trek to the *mango bush*. It seems like an old cultural rendezvous where people seek other than *hairy-*mangoes. Whenever a woman went to these bushes there were always raised eyebrows. People believed there are some amorous securities in a vegetation blanket. It is so true that people behave differently in the woods. Shadows recalled the stance and approach of the spiritually inclined ganja smoking Hindi...calling "Eh, Fatty..." to the pretty young Asiatic-looking girl walking on the narrow tract passing him. He was carefully "trying a thing"— making an approach; although his wife and home was just around the corner. He certainly was no wolf in the Little Red Riding Hood's tale. He was a sheepish barefooted-Black pussycat trying to toy with a young and beautiful sly cat. There were always whispers of sexual impropriety among heterosexuals. On the streets you would hear the rowdy vendors talking about same sex as: "Mi hear say him a *b-man* or him (they meant she) is a *saddamite.*" No, it does not means being part of the Iraqi president, Saddam Hussein's inner circle! Everything then was a secret, and no one wanted to be considered the corruptor of the young; not even the outrageous Calypsonians singing "What is catty...big boy asked?" There was a high level of respect between individuals. Even the crassest person would never openly discussed private events in public. The exception was the occurrence that took place in a city church where the perpetrator was actually well known...

Then again, the cool Hindi was not as insistent as the matriarchal Church Mother who sexually harassed the young country church sister throughout the night. You hear the word "Saddamite" but had no idea what it meant. It was one of those whispering words, even by the most outlandish market *higglerish-type*. It was just not polite to openly say it. The little frightened Church sister was saved when the cock crows. The crowing cock was not belonging to the harasser. The church sister did emphasize that the Mother definitely had no cock to crow. Apparently she raised only hens! The poor timid sister was too afraid to go outside during the night. She did not know where she was; the big city was just too scary. During the night they voiced their opinions in their tussling dialogue:

"I rebuke you in the name of the Creator!" "He created us all and he knew our wishes too." "But we are women!" "That is why I want you. It was ordained so. Say Shibboleth and come home to me my little country church sister..." "I don't know any such

55

word!" "Give me access!" "No, you are a fallen angel…"

When this event was reported to the Church deacon; he laughed, but this is definitely no joke. It was very confusing. Shadows remembered laughing just to be polite and respectful but he grew up then in realizing that there are others out there with different sexual urges. The crowing cock and the light of day saved this weary unsuspecting woman from a sexual predator operating under the mask of righteousness. This was not a huge international theocratic hegemony where the Bishop could cover up their sexual predators by sending them away. The Church Mother was still there feigning righteousness and preying on her unsuspecting victims. The whispering of incestuous relationships was also there… An older boy from Shadows' school mentioned an outrageous affair with a cousin while sleeping on his uncle's floor after the hurricane. The tale of this forbidden affairs between cousins frightened Shadows and his young friends. He asked if his skin didn't feels creepy, the former schoolmate replied no…he avoided the former schoolmate over the years. It was his first experience that such things could really occur. You read about those in books and hear the often repeated, but considered ridiculous notion that the Royal family married each other, but as a young person you really find those attitudes ridiculous. It came home first hand when a rumor was clarified. He observed an older man, a brown-skinned family friend squeezing his daughter's breast. The child was so comfortable with this arrangement that Shadows decided never to visit them again. The father invited him but did not wish him visiting a second time. It was fashionable then (and perhaps even now) that many families wanted people of a *specific* color around their families. This "red-skinned" incestuous family believed they were high-class aristocrats. An example of this is when the man's wife referred to a Black in-law who tried helping her as, "You are bad breed people; you can do that." To Shadows surprise the in-law did not say a word. But why should he; the man had been conformed by his parent's long ago to bow to the wishes of the pigmentation power.

"Ways of the Island's *plantocracy* as they tried to maintain and purify (or putrefies) their pigmentation power!

These were the days when the Newspaper articles were deeply concerned about lewdness. The popular song then, "What is catty, Big boy asked?" was joked at as "what is lewdness?" During those days there was a concentrated outcry about the book "Lady Chatterly's Lover," the D. H. Lawrence's book that caused terrible social upheavals elsewhere. These were the days before the open sexual revolution. The book was banned on the island, of course; so were numerous movies with racial overtones.

The great actor Sidney Poitier then started coming in positive roles. (His name was pronounced like *porter*, the sweet wholesome, organic drink from certain roots...) Back then, even the movie "Blackboard Jungle" was considered a threat! There were numerous so-called "under-16" movies that were so infantile. Movies with positive portrayal of Blacks were a threat...unless it was some childish Bible espousing scene where some hefty Black woman is always looking skywards and praying. At these scenes people in the movies, especially the guys from the "Fowl Roost," the lower sections, usually cuss out these characters by telling them to "...go away wid dem expletive dey!" It was obvious what the rulers wanted. The young apolitical Shadows usually wondered why the patrons are so irreverent. A friend from the "mid section" one night said, "How come they never show any of the pretty White women praying and going on like that. You believe is so all a dem American Black woman look and *galang* — behaved?" Censorship was everywhere, and so was the propaganda of "*we are better than they are....*" The worst movie he had ever seen was the silly moronic Good Friday movie called, "Blood of Jesus"....with the classic racial overtones of the simple Blacks giving their imagery of the scared bulging eyed, acceptable politically indoctrinated performances. Good Friday was the time when all these church restrained right wing Christian types had their excuses to go to the movies and wailed (in the spirit!) And that was good too; shout and be spiritually free in the movie house or wherever!

Living in a rural community does not prepare anyone for city life with its numerous microcosmic "levels of social players" with their identity crisis of where to belong. In the towns, there were little maid servants feigning high-class social acceptance after work. In every tenement yards there were jovial conversations about the new city dwellers type-castes as country boys. There was absolutely nothing on the streets except political discussions or playing "draft game" —checkers at some shop fronts. There were different levels of this game at various shop fronts, but the greatest player in town was "Slew, *the multi-dimensional shifter*." This man was a shopkeeper who made his living selling ice, making barrels and selling other nix-nax. He was a high level player with some tricky insights on the checkerboard. A beautiful checkerboard (draught board) was always laid out under the eaves of Slews' old shop. This was a challenge to the World to come and play whether you are a good player or not. If you are a very poor player you could be laughed at though; so know your limitation and stay away. There definitely was no gambling here, it was a purist game. And it was near the police station too. The old guys hanging around were high level players also. One sunny day a stranger, slender, and neatly dressed young man of a lighter shade with a couple of his friends showed up unannounced. It was obvious none of these guys had ever done any hard work in their lives. The slender young man sat down at the draft board, choosing the black players. His friends stood behind him and they patiently waited without exchanging a word. Slew's friends closed ranks and waited for something to happen. There was silence. It was indeed a challenge, but by whom? This begins Slews greatest contest against the young undefeated city wizard, "Killsome, *the final summation*," from Kingston. Killsome quickly zigzagged through Slews' defensive matrix, running up a quick 3-love game, an unheard of score until then. The "summation" turns the "multidimensional" defense into a coarse sieve. Slew's friends inwardly weep that Killsome was about to slay "Slew" with a 6-love, an unheard of idea at that time. The "Slew" marshaled his own defenses and unravels the "summations'" serpentine cell to cell mosaic shift. He then sets up a labyrinth of defensive moves and drew 23 consecutive games to stumble the young wizard. Some of Killsome's moves were daring with high degrees of unpredictability. It was as if he was sourced into storages of easily look-ahead tables; just accessing the moves as he goes along. He was fast and at times seemed to be unbalanced as if hop scotching between parallel universe while trying to break the rhythm of the wily and more orthodox Slew's new found strangulation on his offense. The "Slew" then wins 3 consecutive games with some masterful shifting plays. The young Killsome got up and stretched, mentally summarized many of Slews moves, and then neatly do a mosaic shift to imperil Slews' new found offense, resulting in numerous stalemates. He drew 19 consecutive games going into the midnight. Slew then put Killsome's tricky serpentine offense on ice by "barreling" (contained) his wily and unorthodox opponent motion with a chilling defense. As Slew's defense emerged the versatile Killsome would still use numerous new summations to contort himself free. Finally the weary old draft-playing guys stepped in and ask both players to consider the match a draw...they were perhaps making certain that no one ever beats Slew in their life time, especially some young wizard from the big competitive city!

Shadows remember that during this game no one ate. Not even the spectators. People were quiet and respectful. One woman whispered that her husband should come home to dinner because the game was nearly over. Her husband just looked at her as if saying

Slew is playing his heart out, do you think we should leave him now. They just looked at each other with an insight in their special privacy, and held hands watching the game to the end… Yes, that was a game of opposites but with no hint of anger or cheating; mental adroitness was the order of the day. Good game guys…

"Drop-pan"—number vendors — and players were everywhere. Then there were the usual "Number dreamers" giving what they called a "rake"—or hint, on, which number would play. The drop-pan players place great emphasis on the mystique of a child's dreams. In this social mix reside the harried cane field workers, none living-in maidservants, handcart-pushers and everyone in the lower social mix. After the crop-over *corchy* sounds, the cane crop mercifully ends, releasing the tired workers to a well-deserved state of physical regeneration. In this period of rest returns economic scarcity when most parents made *"fashions"*—mixing and cooking whatever you have to feed their family. We are not thinking of cooking a "bella-gut pot"—big pot, we are complimenting the skillfulness of the nurturing parents who went the distance when the road was rough whether their cooking utensils were "yabba"—crock pot, or "dutch pots." This is about riding out the economic storm, and had nothing to do with keeping up with the neighbors in a "long eye" way— envying other people's belongings. Just bear in mind though that "yabba" cooking was cool! If you are a "yabba" cooking person you should have the delicate touch of the cool breeze on a smiling face during a quiet starlit night…Now, use your "turn stick"—wooden stirrer, and stir on with the "leggings"—seasonings in your beef soup. Shadows at this time noted that most children were routinely treated as inferiors…and given the worst part of the meal. He always wonders about this behavior…but was made to understand the bread winner must be well fed… The contrary thing here though is; if the breadwinner is a female she does not take the best part of the meal. Am I missing something here? Common sense and respect!

Then there were the quiet and careful huddled whispers of communicable diseases between young people. His older street-wise friends engaged him in a discussion that people with communicable diseases gave the hospital alias names to hide their identities. The joke is whenever their names are called; sometimes they cannot remember their aliases. Shadows visited one of these hospitals by mistake. He was told to sit on a bench and wait. The usual waiting routine for these public hospitals… There were many expectant looking men sitting on long benches. They all acted friendly but very cautious. No one wanted to give eye contact, or to talk. This was definitely not a place for a popularity contest! He noticed an immaculately dressed nurse came out and made strong eye contact with him. He strongly held his position in this contest. She walked back into another room and returned with two other nurses. They whispered and again looked at Shadows. He heard some one said, "They are all here." The well dressed nurse then whispers in dismay; "Even that little one too!" Shadows had just wanted a blood test, because there were numerous adolescent pimples breaking out on his face. The *wisdom* (yikes!) then was you have *bad blood*. In that case you either drink *hallows and porter*—an extremely bitter concoction, or get a blood test to verify if you had something else. During those days no one generally knows what kills anyone. People just die. In other words, "Him dead you know!" "Woee mi gad and him was such a good man?" "Mi hear say a dem obeah him fi whe him have." Then there was always: "Mi dream say…" after that discussion. Be aware that the general cultural mindset was (is?) that no one ever dies unless someone killed them.

Anyway, the nurse was relieved when she gave the direction to another building for the blood testing. "Praise God!" she repeated looking towards the heavens. Shadows defiantly inquired, "Praise God for what?" The nurse gave a winning smile and motherly shoo him on saying, "Go on, go on…Teddy come on, show him where the place is quick." She definitely wanted him to leave quickly. He believed then that this was the mysterious *"lying-in"* –deliver room section at the hospital. In his childlike world that place was one of the great mysteries. He recalls how nervous men were always whispering and secretly vanishing to take presents to their women at these mysterious "lying-in" places. He was now wondering how come so many frightened men were there without presents. Anyway, at that time he satisfied his thoughts that the men already gave their presents and was awaiting something else. It was years later that Shadows understood the nurse's surprise. In those days sex was the ultimate mystery; therefore "big people" and children, or adolescent cannot have any such discussion. The word "sex" was never used. If the meaning of the word was ever implied it was some foolish euphemism as "sheg," "dweet" or "rudeness." No wonder Shadows little cousin; decades later came home crying that her little friend, "Dinner Bell," told her he was going to *saca saca* her! She said she did not know what the word means but it definitely sounded outrageous. Well it sounds childish now, but just imagines if someone should approach you, and petitioned to *saca saca* you. How you would feel when he pointed to some tree in the darkness and said:

"...come ya gal mek mi saca saca you under that tree over there when we ah come back from the shop!"

Such are the sounding of words, even without the body language. Even now Shadows jovially wonders if his dear little cousin heard what little Dinner Bell had said. He knows his loving second cousin perhaps had one of those hidden "paper-cigars" with her, not to smoke but to probably light her way while returning from the store in the darkness according to her... Or probably they both had paper cigars! They always have these excuses whenever they are caught smoking. "Me was playing with it like the Bauxite chu chu train that passes here." "But my dear little cousin the train that passes here is a diesel..." "But it has smoke too." She got you on that one, so you just smile, and asks her to carefully throw away the paper cigars...knowing that she possibly have a few backup cigars in the other frock pocket too. Shadows reflected on the many times they are caught shuffling under the cool mango trees near the stand pipe during their smoke off, trying to pass it off as playing "Peas porridge hot, peas porridge cold..." whenever an adult is seen coming their way. There were always these family prayers that they *don't burn down the place* whenever they are left by themselves… "Watch them, they cannot be trusted by themselves…!" Or words to that effect.

Shadows recalls returning from work and seeing his friend tightly covered up in bed. Shadows was surprise because his friend seems to be in robust health when he left for work that morning. At least Shadows believed so. His friend started explaining that he went to the hospital for a penicillin injection to cure his illness. After the injection he fainted and was taken home and sent to bed. Shadows immediately understood where he was during the "blood testing" incident. He had heard many whispering about sexually transmitted diseases. Now he reflected how strange it was that there was no information on this topic in schools or in the newspapers. (Are these people in any way related to the Africans who deny having an AIDS epidemic?) Of course no one then ever openly discussed any thing sexual. They only got angry if someone got pregnant. Information definitely was not their forte. They either did not have it; or they did not know how to use it. But what can one ever expect from a people who would not even tell their children their own ages, their parents' ages or real names, or family structures. *"A whe you a ask fi you age- paper for? A woman you a tun pon me!"* Some parents have what is called a "doctor book"—-a book on human physiology and medical terms, which is hidden away under lock and key somewhere in the house from their growing children! The contrary thing is that the pale-skinned ones are more prone to release information to their young. Can you see the correlation here with information, power, and domination relative to the pigmentations?

During this time there were numerous opened liaisons between the sexes. He recollected the incident with two of his older friends. In those days everyone wanted to be a *"face man,"* or a *"face girl"*— means to be beautiful to look at. And that is all you may get too! One of the friends left his sweater in a dance. He went back to retrieve it. In his absence, the adroit *"face man"* friend went away with his friend's newly found girl friend. He claimed he *late* him. They almost ended up quarrelling. Unfortunately after a few weeks later, the cool *"later" face man* needs some special medication. This incident repeats itself in another scenario when two friends went to pick up two girls. The arranger of the pickup has a car so he demanded the prettier girl. Yes, owning a transport has its merit, just ask any taxi operator on the island. He too ended up seeing the medic's face. Perhaps the old Calypsonian knew a few things, that is why he is singing *gives matrimony to a ugly woman, if you wanted to be happy for the rest of your life...*

Shadows recollects the talkative young man in the neighboring tenement yard coming from his room and loudly proclaiming:

"Me say, me wean long time ago, so me no need no more milk."

All the "big people" immediately became taut in their faces, frowning at his adolescent outspokenness. Shadows never then understood the statement. He was smart enough by then not to ask when he looked at the adults' rigid faces and their fierce body languages...with their usual culturally unspoken, "You asked too much questions!"

DANCES

In those days buses had defined routes, with names like Magnet, Sunshine, Enterprise (Old British recycled buses that were always breaking down.), Western Flyer, and Bronx. "Higglers" were first transported to the market in opened top trucks, and later by improved covered trucks. Sunday outings by chartered buses, trains and trucks were prevalent.

A guy could spend the whole Sunday evening polishing up his bicycle to promenade on Sunday evenings before going to the movies. In those days owning a bicycle, especially a decorated one was a big thing. The Rudge and Raleigh bicycle Sport models were the rage then. People were always asking to go on bicycle joy-rides. Perhaps modern day China is like this now! Who then could really afford to buy cars? There were actually no other common and easily accessible means of transportation then. The naughty response, "A drive for a ride!" could be the response whenever a woman asked for a bicycle ride. The word "towing" was used to mean someone riding with you on a bicycle.

This was the time before the first Sunday dance at the New Yorker Club, a private club, which caused so much religious outrage and guilt. In this context of rage he remembers the ultimate adolescent embarrassment when a dancing partner lost her "crinoline" dress while doing some fancy twirling. "Christmas walk" during the early morns of mid-December were a favorite past time for the young. Parents were afraid of this too, no, not bandits; it was child bearing fears! During this time Rock and Roll music was coming into its own. The Sound Systems started to emerge, changing the whole musical landscape. These sound systems have specific followers and definable names like Ruddys, Birdland, Coxson's Downbeat and King Edwards's. The new generation was hooked on the American music. Every sound system has its top cadre of dancers or "legs man" and woman too. Eventually there was no battle of the favorite bands; it was the battle for supremacy of the new electronic music giants as they try "stamping" out each other. A typical contest would have each system trying to play a "good" song that the opponent did not have. Everyone would be dancing and listening while shouting "Stamp Out!" whenever one system failed to live up to expectation. The emergence of the *sound systems* changed social etiquette. People were dancing more freely without the old social shackles. According to the older generations, manners became coarser. Then older folks always lament the social behavior of the younger group: "When we were growing up we never acted so rude." You could say there was more openness in gyration, or as they called it "rubbing and scrubbing." The "older set" categorized the new dance styles as "dem a whine up *pon* one another." The music was definitely louder with more variety. The other favorable thing was the continuity of the playing time. There was no drunken and unruly musician taking a long break to quaff another *qq*— quarter quart of rum or to proposition his new favorite woman in the darkness outside. Shadows recalled his neighbor, "Rude Bwoy" McDonald from across the scene, dancing and gyrating out of control to the Rock and Roll beat at Prison Oval where a lady commanded him to buy her a drink. You see, she counted the number of times they danced without drinking. The contrite "Rude Boy" gladly bought the drink because he was enmeshed within her dancing *gyrations*... It should be pointed that the "rude boy" label was actually attached to anyone who decided to be cool and stay a little outside the stifling social norms. You did not have to be flashing your dangerous "ratchet knife," and singing that *"rude bwoy come from jail,"* one of the hot local hits. Oh, yes, this was way before the rampant "ragamuffin style" and its social setbacks...

Dance admission fees for women were less than men were. People enjoyed dancing in the dark...and their deeds were not evil. There was not much available cash during that time. "The woman a sweat so buy her a beer nuh!" was the general outcry from the more socially responsive older guys. Forget about women buying their own drinks. Some did not even want to pay their own fares. On the other hand, some of the older guys were tricky. They wished to impress the younger women and take her away from the "uncouth" poorer and younger guys. Just be careful of their graciousness... It seems every woman liked drinking Milk Stouts, a status symbol. The simplest alcoholic drink in those days got the people drunk. The population was not used to alcoholic drinks. Rum had its devil label and for some beer was too long. The population was lemonade and carrot juice drinkers. Shadows found this out the hard way when his friend had to take home a drunken in-law. Dances away from the City were considered fashion statements. They could be dangerous also. The country men could get belligerent...so a *town man* had to be tactful. In visiting a dance in St. Mary he confronted the dangerous situation of trying to show up a country man with your fancy town-moves. These big muscled guys and their friends would stand in a dim corner glaring at you! Just watching how many times you are dancing with their admirers… not necessarily their lovers. The next time he may come over and claimed you "mashed his toes" without saying excuse. Shadows reminisces about the incident with a big muscled guy in his lily-white merino and fancy pants; with this woman tailgating and wiping his brow with her beautiful handkerchief. All this was contrived to show off the dominant *country-peacock*. Shadows had his fancy kerchief also. No, Shadows handkerchief was not hanging half-way out of his back-pocket; that would be overkill, just too radical a show for what was supposed to be a calm country scene. Big-muscled looked at Shadows, smiling, and said, "You are all right; you dancing with my sister"— a permission to feel secure. Why not, Shadows was treating his sister with respect. Undoubtedly this well fed guy was the pampered "local bully." A young man must also know the dance hall economics politics too. This is a free loading policy where drinking buddies call their friends to drink at your expense. This is generally done to the younger guys. There was not many mention of birth control, so responsible men had to be very careful… Yes, there were whispers of diseases too; so know when to say no to the women too. He remembered being neatly dressed into his cool "pepper-seed" pants, dancing moccasin and blue Arrow shirt when a naughty lady made a proposition towards the river bank. Although they were a bit drunk; he found it inappropriate to comply because of the drizzling rain and the probability of a scandal at his old school. Months later she passed his home. She was very pregnant. He realized then that she was pregnant at the dance. He asked her about it. She blatantly replied, "I came there especially to give you it, but you were too smart." How undeservingly friendly...!

Cultural music then becomes a pariah as the young move away from the "mentos" and the calypso songs. The older folks were still reminiscing about the elite *quadrille* dance...although the Spaniards had long left the island's dancing scene. During this period emerged new dress codes. The men started wearing different color shirts, where generally they would wear only white shirts. The women became more radical and started wearing off-the-shoulder tops, showing the bare back and firm bust line. The Generation gap battle between the older women and the younger more daring women were fierce. Of course the churches got involved with numerous weak minded and cowed men joining in calling the women names; although they admire the ladies bare backs. Just wait until during the nights at the movies and dances to see their magnified adorations. The new dance craze was called "Yanking." Some doctor was reputed to have a sign in his hospital, the only one in the area stating; "No bed for Yankers." Years later they caught him on the floor, almost naked with someone other than his wife. Is this more serious than yanking? It was a time when cool youngsters wear their "bugga"—ankle high flannel-type shoes with rubber soles to the dance. Here again, it was reasoned that only worthless and very low class people wear "*crept,*" – forerunner to the tennis shoes, *or* "bugga;" although no one would buy a shoeless person a shoe. They still shunned them when they are barefooted. The general feeling was that bugga wearing was dangerous, because the wearer walked too softly—you can't hear them coming, and only thieves walked that way. The trendy and radical young *bugga-bops* types spend hours, applying whitening to their *buggas* to bop the weekend nights away. Bugga and dancing was just too cool and radical for the conservative and class conscious population. It was a joke seeing some of these tie-wearing guys sweating like fat little pigs in their tightly drawn ties and closely fitting coats in the broiling sun. "I am a decent person!" according to the British standards. At this time many men wear short pants. It was about this time that young boys were introduced to long pants. *Long pants* were generally scripted for mature men. A boy wearing long-pants would be considered a "forced-ripe man"—precocious, and opened to the challenging query, "Boy you think you are a man!" One such boy answers that query by asking, "You think you are a woman wearing short panty?" The questioner was absent for weeks; the next time he came out wearing *old iron blue* long pants. Schoolboys started the long pants revolution by teasing and playfully slapping other boys on the knees with the comment, "Cover your knees." Years later Shadows read where some behaviorists had later commented that the short pants wearing was not purely for reasons of economics and, or comfort. It was preconceived as a tool to show the Black masses are simple children …a little Darwinism!

Hustling was everywhere… During the Christmas and Easter holidays there were big fairs and dances.

The religious people find a way to make money by having people tossing hoops over bottle of jams or other preservatives. A disgruntled customer, after many near misses made a test by matching the hoops around the stands on which the bottle sits. He had to force the hoop over the stand so there is no way he could have won a bottle of jam. So deceptive, how could anyone wins a prize? (By miracle you say, "…because…all things are possible." Good!) Was this theft? The booth attendant apologized, and unwillingly decided to give him a bottle. He was not to keen to accept. The young Shadows shed his idealism, and lost his respect for the organizers of that booth, although he was a member of that organization. He really felt sorry for the booth attendant, but he knew the "organization" had been cheating people for many years with those bottles of preservatives—how mean spirited.

The big movers on the scene were the tradesmen and the businessmen; they rule the roost… All types of underhand "swapping" takes place because resources were not readily available to everyone. A certain businessman decided "swapping" a pair of shoes for a woman's "special" favors. In the darkness he gave her one foot of shoe and a bottle in the box to prevent the contents from rattling. Later, she returns saying he made a mistake in the darkness, by putting an empty beer bottle instead of the shoe. Games people play? He *wholeheartedly* apologized and requested "another run at their play." Both have their requests granted with smiles, and everyone is forgiven …until another time, perhaps…

Then on the other side there were those country business people who wanted to play in the big city. We see what happens when a popular country-boy businessman comes to town and try to use country tricks in the towns…he nearly drown. Women showing their legs were practically forbidden. No they were not Moslems obeying the Sharia law; they were just afraid to be free! Therefore there are a few women who can swim. Imagine being surrounded by water but unable to swim. The society seems more threatened that "de gal a show him leg!" than being able to stay afloat. On one occasion a woman took this country-man on her back far out in the sea to an old concrete construction. The man could not swim. While there his romantic desires got the better of his sense for survival. He tried being romantic a few times and she gently refused him. He became a bit forceful. (Could have been the ozone in the sea air mixing with her beautiful tantalizing semi-nude dark body). She asked him if he can swim. He replied no. (He failed to understand the warning!) On his next try she flipped him off the concrete ledge; held him under water for a few times then calmly asks him if he was ready to go ashore. He cried like a drowning man, which he was, and pleaded with her that he would behave. She took him safely back to shore. He hastily ran for his clothe and find his way off the beach ignoring all her pleas that they should first make love before he goes home. The non-swimmer lost his sense of priority: he wants to forcefully make love in deep water where he has no control. But refused to calmly accept some loving on land where he has more control. What a confusing situation… Going to the beach was like a watery invitation to go to the mango bushes. An incident at Port Henderson reminds Shadows of the similarity. There is also a very concrete difference. The sea is water; the bush is land. If you forget this you may *not* live to remember it. He is reminded about the man in the broken canoe, and also the scandal on the beach... The Port Henderson incident implied: If you cannot swim do not try *trespass* on others watery affairs. They may just leave you at sea! And after that there could be either a burial, or scandal on the beach.

There were always some scandals on the streets. Many accident-prone people think they were cagey, and always looking for privacy in the wrong place. They lived in a small town and believed that having a rendezvous at any of these hotels in town will give them privacy. An astute business man asked his woman to buy goods in the City. He then trailed her to her hotel rendezvous. He went to her so-called private room and caught her in the act. He calmly unsheathed his weapon; rolls back the sheets while cutting his finger nails, and then quietly requested his money by saying: *"Chuoh man! Since that you busy, just give me the money and stay and enjoy yourself."* The poor lady had never been seen again. No, no, he did not kill her! But it was so obvious that the *"two old fires ticks easy to ketch again"* would not occurs after she dropped out of circulation. She was intelligent, attractive and nice, quite loving too. This man was as cool as his uncle, the Pharaoh, the leader of the family through the hard times. *Shadows recalled when his uncle's* girlfriend took him to court because of a melt down in their business deal. She won the case and they came home laughing and had beers together. When a surprised Shadows asked how come they are drinking together; the Pharaoh tersely replied, "It was a business project." He quickly realized their relationships were about money, not sexuality. Later Shadows saw the downside to all these sexual forays was unwanted children and misery. Then there is the "*water rate*" case; the legal condition where the women asks the courts for child maintenance. To many men that was worse than marriage because numerous times these baby relationships were purely speculative... The judge would command the men to maintain a child, or sentence him to prison if he did not pay although he has no money or job! Shadows recalls a mother lamenting about her ex-lover as "*Him and his Jimmy swing gal them*" has caused her mental anguish. He never understood what "Jimmy swing gal" was; but he saw her face and understood her anguish. It seems he abandoned her with her young child for another younger woman. This type of abandonment is also done by the females too...they gave their children to some grand parent, or "paperless" adoptive person and just carelessly "walks away" to another man claiming: "*Mi soon come.*" There is no logical thinking, love or intuitive awareness, just the *leggo beast*-type of Tantric exercises. An old naughty woman once explained: "De man dem heart is willing to change, but their flesh is "erect" so de woman dem give them what dem want." Using the age old concept of blaming the male for every thing bad! To counter this, a fierce street "Arab" vendor was so fed up with being hustled for his hard earned cash that he shouted to his mercenary female admirer (hustler?); "Move your bosomy self from off my hand or I will take a righteous stand." True sah! Some time though, you definitely have to obey a Higher Order and take another stand!

CHAPTER 7

"STRIKE'S" PHILOSOPHY

During this time period everyone has their encounter groups, even the gamblers too. A boy perhaps learnt most things from the men outside his family. There were street philosophers with good knowledge of international and local events. The man, "Strike" was one of these types, who were just not main stream people from the gentry's upscale, country club, old boy types. Those from the upscale groups were too pigmentation conscious to offer help without exacting a servile price from the Blacks!

Shadows can still remember the quality discussions between Pancho and "Strike!" the Hill Reader. Strike was always acting as if he was some witty Zen Master dealing in some types of spiritual abstraction... He believes in American pragmatism of money being the driving force for everything. He went on farm work in the early 1940's and was impressed with the American way of life. After that he vowed he would never go to any other place where the British flag flies. He believed they were all similar to the hardships experienced on the island. He had never mentioned *separate but equal.* Perhaps he did not see that being practiced on Jim Crow's farms. Pancho on the other hand believes in honor. Their main discussion was: "What do you prefer honor or money?" Strike always maintained if you have money you can have honor, can even buy it too. But if you have honor you can die for wants as most soldiers did after the government heap honor on them after the wars. Pancho maintains you cannot buy honor because the honorable is not for sale. These men were from different social backgrounds. Pancho was the brown skinned colonialist city type, which had traveled to Cuba and had all the social advantage, whereas Strike the Hill Reader was the bright dark skinned suburban type with a better level of education. Shadows remembered listening to these two guys philosophically go at it. Things were so contrary then, because their chief referee was a compulsive gambler named "Smoked-out," an excellent tradesman who was always without money. This person was the first human Shadows knew that deals in social excesses. He never could keep money. Whenever he has money he would run away seeking some gambling den. "Smoked-out" was the local diplomat. He knew his existence depends on the good graces of both men, but he too had a strong personality as he walked the tight rope of not offending his two socially stabled companions. He once defined his life's parameter as, "A man born as a man can't dead as a pig!" Meaning he will never succumbed to a level lower than his innate humanity. It seems that he finally got his wishes by leaving town and redeemed himself through Christianity.

Strike likes smokes and philosophy. Shadows spent hours listening to the "mentor"'s traveling experiences coupled with some of his spicy sexual exploits. Prior to this, no one had ever discussed sexual situations with Shadows. Pancho once mentioned that Strike's stories were about prostitutes. Strike came back and asked Pancho if Cuba was not used as a whorehouse for the

Americans. Pancho was alarmed! The silence that follows gave the young Shadows the feeling that these guy's discussions were not too friendly. Over the years it played out that one was for the entrenched social order; whereas the other one was for a changing social order.

Over the years The Mentor foolishly got sidetracked by one of the numerous street mercenaries and surprisingly *committed* an offense. An event that is shocking to Shadows, that solicits the response, "What is wrong with these acquaintances with knives?" It seems that the mean streets will eventually exact a price if you stay too long on its unsavory paths as happened to both Big Dog Roy and then Strike! Both were farm workers that had their eyes opened to a different social reality on the American farms. They were not some silly proponents of the American trashy ghetto lingo of the returning farm workers. He recalled Roy's happiness at West Parade on the returning truck, when he confused Shadows by acting American. He then laughed saying, "Look at your face; you expects me to come back with 'conked' hair and twanging!" They both greeted each other and laughed at the spectacle…. This was before the "Mentor" hid from the law in a cave where he met a caring barefooted food carrying woman. It seems after numerous months of helping him she demanded his "use" as payment— he had no "loot" left then! Apparently, their "communication" evoked her comment, "Boy you can *sheg* sweet you know!" In looking back, it seems family politics drove the mentor away from home, when he mistakenly believes a mother is the only one to trust in the family. Is this an Island idea, or the

Black group's misconception that your mother will save your money for you if you send it to her? What happens to the banks? Is this an old island excuse for failure…heard it so many times…particularly specific to the English immigrants? Again, this could be a legacy from slavery where the moms may be the only nurturing base for the family, or likely just the legacy of motherhood…or just being incompetent by not getting enough information on how to accomplish things?

Irrespective of what, all due respect; another salute to a friend and a salute to the Mentor also…

Shadows remembers his first meeting with the Mentor. It was through an insult to the family. "All of them is just one big *three-twelve!*" This was a serious alphabetically-coded insult in those days. After that family insult was smoothed over, Shadow's uncle asked the mentor to keep Shadows for a weekend when the family left town. The mentor took him to the ganja-smoking den at Tawes Pen. The vendors here were never easily raided because of their neighborhood cooperation. They constantly watch each other's property. This may have been the first Neighborhood Watch on the island. And it is of an inverse social order too: watching out for the police to enable the neighborhood to be continually safe to commit a crime. It was here that he first openly observed adults using ganja. The old dealer puts it under an old discarded *chimmy* or more politely called a chamber pot on the road embankment, a short distance from her house. (Like, yes, keep the illicit goods in the government domain; let them charge themselves!) A faded old red cloth among the brushes covered this old rusty and chipped pot. On further observation it appears as if the clothes were some filthy, old discarded ladies garment. No one wants to touch that…not even the raiding police. Such could brand you with a nasty nickname. The seller had a good view of her trade from all angle of her home. When a buyer comes she would not take the money unless she knows you. She would also deny she is a trader if you were a stranger. Even if you were a loyalist she would ask you to *look under that chimmy and you may find something there.* To pass the money you will have to drop it on the ground and walk away. That is before you look under the old rusty *chimmy.* She would walk away with you too, and then return for the money on the ground with the exclamation that she found some money on the ground. She would first ask you if it is your money…you should say no! In that case the police had legal problem infiltrating the trade. It is said that there is force behind every authority; well here there is force behind every businesswoman. These people had no desire to go to prison so they would physically fight the police to escape. It was never good tactics to confront them in their homes. There were no computer keeping tabs on the citizens in those days, once they escaped from custody there were problems tracing them because everybody have bogus names and address! It was considered disgraceful in having a prison record, or even going to jail. Going to debtor's jail was a bit different. To place someone in Debtor's Jail you had to pay their accommodating expenses to keep them in jail. He remembers the "Big people" talking about someone being placed in Debtor's Jail. They made it sounds that the debtor was having a good time wearing his white shirt and tie, and ordering his newspaper, ham and bacon, and coffee every morning. And this was all at the plaintiff's expense! When Shadows asked for clarification; he was told this type of jail is only for the genteel types... Imagine doing that now!

CHAPTER 8

VLLAGE POLITICS: A HEALER COMES TO JUDGEMENT

After all these years, he has returns to another remote village, although now there is an international saying that "the world is becoming a single village." Is this one-village concept, a dangerous one or what! Someone once said, "Don't just come across my fence with your pretty "bancra" —straw type handbag — picking my fruits that you did not plant; telling me you are my neighbor from the World's Village." Agreed, they may want to have some *"brawta"*—a few more— fruits as friendly gesture also. This so-called global Village according to the social activists is working against people's privacy. On the other hand globalization seems to removes the stifling secrecy that corrupt systems used to mistreat its citizens. An educated mass could banish the general apathy that perpetrated ignorance and the crippling fear of making radical changes from the ineffective legacies of past colonial governments. Unfortunately we have not seen much of these worthwhile changes…

Her story continues, and she is telling him about the usual male "gender compliance" politics of calling strong willed independent women lesbians. A ruse to force women to abandon their hopes, and comply with the popular male vision of the inept females. She called them a group of *pianh-pianh*—feeble minded men trying to take away every independent woman's dream. On the other hand women used the similar tactics in ensnaring eligible men who showed no personal interests in them. Women too played the gender name calling game to inveigle men to show that they are virile...an economical entrapment on their part.

Shadows met some of the Healer's friends, and were puzzled by the reaction from one of her well connected associates. This beautiful lady was somewhat playfully "higglerish-like" noisy, with a penchant towards adolescent behaviors of trying to incur jealousy among the group by using her economic power. Shadows became wary when he notices her using old childish teenaged group strategy on a more aware and older group. The lady went to her cultural roots, and with vengeance resurrected the old district social routines to impress her disadvantaged friends, and thereby help maintain her influence in the district. It appears the old-time social class Village culture still plays a pivotal role with this expatriate. It was always said that traveling broadens the mind, oh so contrary here; it seems to narrows the focus of some pretty would be village leader! Someone probably had never heard the urbane phrase, "If you move you lose." In the world of human sexuality some things still remain constant, sexual attraction coupled with economic power. Shadows enjoyed her associate's tantalizing and skillfully organized exposures: white attractive *clothes*, bathing suit affairs, and sensuous body oiling rituals. Were these daring postures her clinic of attraction and tools of conformity. Were these tools and episodes used without the desired effect? To successfully use a message one has to be aware of it, and accepts it. But then, how can one be searching for a mystical path but still choose to stay on the old defeatist egoistic ways of believing the love for money transcends all things? In their affairs, Shadows tries to determines if she made mistakes, or the *errors* were being deliberately contrived? If it is not contrivance, then, does a spiritual seeker becomes obsessed with the demise of others? And, then why being so angry, and being so evasive when confronted with the truth? Shadows asks himself, "What are the parameters for a true evaluation of this behavior?" He recollects their *discussion* in the room…the *silence* between parties at her home…the message of *departure time; a departure* that was never done. Did he fail to read the warning message then? He evaluated her trivial district mantle of control and remembers her shameful treatment of the hungry *Bearded unfortunate* at the Beach. He wonders if this *beautiful tycoon's desire is the using of poor people.* It seems there is a widespread acceptance here that a male doing business with this woman is teetering on the edge of financial destruction. He looks at the hungry man and understands that a policy of self-respect is difficult to maintain on a hungry stomach. This is more so it seems with addicted smokers…a double whammy in that case. Is she aware of her action, or is it a show of power, or one of vengeance for some conceived social slight during her childhood? Such would make those with power looks socially deficient and heartless. Many "wound-up" expatriates return as heartless little uncompromising colonialists who are still mentally lingering in colonial times with their new found "money power." They used the similar behaviors as their Old Colonialist masters

85

of chiding the "none traveled" masses as being lazy and unimaginative. Here again, almost everyone copes by copying the popular sloganeering phrase, "I am a Christian." From all these numerous utterances you would believe they burnt "worldians"—- non-Christians—-at the stakes. The political utterance "It takes a village to raise a child may be true," but when the child reached adulthood, its dependency should decrease. It seems that is a contrary notion is this village. The pretty associate knows her villagers and manipulates them to her wishes by handing out "gifts" tied to her control strings. If anyone resisted her entreaties or command, then it seems the result is slanders and scandals within the Village. Unfortunately her action leads to silly banter songs…

"…all the lies dem a tell me nuh watch that!"

A friendly touch, or sharing of meals on a common utensil— "bird feeding"— can cause an eruption to what was once considered a budding friendship? The end result is now like a mighty Pharaoh comes to judgement after he is being silenced and ostracized by a powerful priest. In this case an irate priestess with a given economical, and "born ya" – born here— with a district birth cultural advantage. What is her agenda here? Materialism rules this Village politics because resources are miserly. Here the often-bantered Christian ethics are just imaginary platitudes that binds little groups into foraging economical forces, which delights in the simple trivial pursuits of gossiping on who is having sex with whom.

Shadows watched the "environmental shapers"— men with machetes, not "small axes," try earning a living by clearing the land to plant crops. He was surprised that the s*lash and burn tactics* is still used in land preparation. It is said that tribes living on the edge of the Sahara used this agricultural practice to their destruction; causing creeping desert where there were verdant plants. The tribes are doing things their parents did for millennium, and are unwilling to change. Scarcity caused people to choose some rough strategy to survive... just merely. Be linked with the past, yes, but famine is not the form of linkage you want to use to reach your fore parent! We need to be focused on a more realistic economic point.... Shadows scrutinized the men working in the hot sun, and trying to avoid land boundary and irritation disputes that can results in petty family politics. He passed the scrutiny in the Village streets by a "church sister" and another more outspoken sister too! The Spirit Healer possible has her life in new fluctuations that warrants a matriarchal sister reminding her that there is another. "So tell me dear little choosy girl what's your game here now? Do you know the Village Idiots are talking about you? Do you want our good family name, your good name to be mud?" The Healer boldly, or according to the rumor-prone Christian Villagers, brazenly walked to church showing her winning smile under the cold scrutiny of her once admiring neighbors. Her *"fire-under-your-feet"* guest as she calls him, had no idea he was walking into a complicated social dilemma. A social morass where the Church still exhibits a Middle Ages power over the ignorant masses! The Villagers espoused the Christian ideas as a psychological **juggernaut** to obliterate any open and friendly gender reaction between people. Shadows thinks how contrary this attitude is to the 21st Century. But is he to tell anyone how to live? The Spirit Healer did her spiritual stuff oblivious of the pending *crucifixion*...or did she know that is why she kept her house door ajar whenever she has a male visitor! There should be a written warning on the Village social principles, stating: "Observe the social and religious Village protocols or expects to be roasted with slanders and scandals!" Every little showing of friendship or love turns into an emotional roller coaster. The social interplay of subtlety, discretion and somewhat indiscretion plays havoc with ones mind. This district is a place where social interplays among the sexes invoke a feeling of guilt where none should exist— definitely a place of theocratic control. A place where ones exhibition of freedom to facilitate an open discussion can lead to another's bondage. This is where hanging out in the dark is fun, but watch out for the wagging tongues in the mornings. So silly, but seems quite predictable here. It would appear that showing love, and, or having sexual desires is foreign here. One wonders how they populate, or they just blatantly copulate? Are they cocks or roosters; hens or pullets? Didn't the Healer rudely point to a body location and say, "Your cock is what caused it!" The *guest* did not know he had one of those because he had not been raising fowls. In this non-discretionary and staid society lived some of the strongest willed women and men. The notable part here is that these people lived alone! An exceptionally strong willed lady "wheel and turn" through the ages on the history of Black philosophy versus economic pragmatism. As she talked and gesticulated through the lessons on color dominance and social reality in a former energetic cane and banana planting economy; Shadows understands the hegemony of the surrounding people who wielded power in this by-passed district. They are no longer here, of course, but their powerless inheritors are still here *floating* on old unearned prestige. Is this similar to the Indian caste system where those who have started it has long disappeared after negatively defining people with socially numbing labels as Hindu Dalita (or Untouchable). These people are now seeking a different status by being converted to Buddhism…imagine changing social and psychological perspective by changing religion. There is no village suggestion of changing color from black to something else. The Black masses in this village and others better realize that knowledge dominates first, not pigmentation. The "other skinned" people obviously knew this. They are ahead first because of their knowledge, not their skin color. Now things in the village have changed, and even the connecting road is no longer traveled by "Timepiece"—the transport bus. The cultural and economic vibrancy are now just history. Shadows can now "look" across time, a time before the "Timepiece," and "sees" and "hears" the old "fife players" in the darkness playing the cultural song,

"…a weh you a wheel a tun mi, a weh you a wheel and tun mi. You want mi fi go fall down, knock mi belly pon tanburina…"

Shadows later "sits in" with a male philosopher who held court in a shop during the cool night. He again marveled at the interpretation and logic of this villager. Indeed, we have lost many of our brilliant people because the social system failed them. Because of this failure to tap our human resources, we as a nation and as a race of people will continue suffering. The slogan—-"be all you can be"—was, and still is not applicable here. He sat in good vibes playing dominoes, and stifles a laugh when a lady called out "Burn them, burn them!" meaning give them "a pass" in the game. He had long ago assimilated the "Burn them" or "bun dem!" call as a defiant Rastafarian's exhortation to power down Babylon—the ruling Western oppressive racist social order. Years ago, no religious thinking "Christian," or main stream social minded person would dare use those words in public. Now it is assimilated as just "control them."

He finally visited one of the village Churches. This is the Spirit Healer's spiritual abode. It was an excellent spiritual experience. The chanting was like a closer touching of Divine Energy. He doesn't know the word; have been told the song and always forget the words but still cannot forget the feeling or the chanting of the tune. Although, he was told there were some tactful observations and probably some later discussions; he saw no merit to give credence to those sensitive people-made concerns. He was there to worship, and he did. He was there as not just a mere churchgoer, but as a spiritualist. Shadows believe that Spiritualists will always rule, and that is in any religion, because all energy emanates and leads to one source—the Creator! The final episode was when the religious court suspends its "witch hunt," or annulled its debate in placing her at what Shadows jovially referred to as the church's "back bench!" It seems a positive decision was made when a group Shadows choose to refer to as the, "Sister Warners" came on the religious prowl and denounced the Caiphas-type tribunal. It was an emotional release for the Spirit Healer.

As he listens to her story, he realized she had been through many things...the discussion continues about her silent defense against a murderous pact of night marauders. It appears they attacked her business place while she lay lonely on her back in the darkness with her gun under her head; listening to the marauders probing the roof after failing to gain access through the doors. Their communications outside were guarded as they tried disguising their voices... At that time their nightly rampage of murder and robbery was unknown to her. But she knew they are armed and with murderous intentions! She stopped and query, "How does a Spiritualist deal with imminent life threatening danger when a weapon is readily available?" Shadows remembers his unspoken question, "Can we then reason, with Death; knowing that once you kill, you do not have the power to undo it?" He did not give a verbal reply...he just patted her shoulder.

Shadows recalled his laying in the darkness too; but under very different circumstances. He is reminded of listening with rapt attention and in silence to the music outside. Even now he can perceptively hears the calling notes of the bamboo fifes that once were played by the vanishing musicians of years gone-by; as they too strolled in the darkness along his quiet village roads. Their names are now uncertain but certainly not their musical prowess. He could not go outside then, and commended them, because he was just a "little boy," and his mother's wishes rule supreme. Those musicians were of his mother's era, therefore they were "big men"—not his companion. Irrespective of that, the notes still entertain Shadows memory. Even now he visualizes the notes forming complex patterns, just flowing throughout the darkness, as he lays there on the verge of sleepiness while basking in the soothing sounds. Yes, he remembers laying in the darkness when no other music was available except the bamboo fife, the banjo or the guitar. Of course there were some of those "other social class" people with their gramophones, with its shrill sounding music (an irrelevant sound then) on some "inaccessible hill tops" where one can merely hear the tune. (Likened to a sign pointing to the island's masses inaccessibility to those who governs...) He recalls voices outside, the "big people" of course, asking who is playing. In later years he met a more radical and mystifying musical group of *frequency conformers...* The *musical ones* went by the group names like Musical Mysticism, which includes *Beyond Flute,* the Mystic Flute, Resonance Flute... He recalled being conformed to listening to their soothing musical notes reverberating throughout the hills. Sometimes one compares hypnotism to a master musician releasing the enjoyable music for others to dance or listen. We dance and make merry without thinking of the musician's feeling of enjoyment. Who ever consider if the artistes get pleasure during the dance? The dancers just selfishly thinks, keep the music playing; play on!

This ingrained selfishness appears to be the reward of many disadvantaged Black women within the society. They contributed to others pleasures and sense of well being but never actually reaped the benefits of their magnificent contributions. Shadows remembers his Auntie who was always there in time of crisis. He recalled how she allows all the Young Pretenders in her family to maintain a sense of dignity. Many of the past Black-generations were victims of abuses in the lower social sphere. They had overcome this social stigma of being Black and considered poor in a racist and class conscious society, even by those whom professed undying friendship during their times of needs. They nourished their families by silently staying in the social shadows, removing obstacles and smoothing the paths for their prideful younger ones. Thank you Auntie for a job well done in helping to banish the lingering darkness of ignorance; and turning the pulsating "inner music" into an euphoric Spiritual response as we march towards the light… You may not be physically here now, but the invisible spiritual and eternal linked bonds are still being felt.

Now he remembers the Marching Bands, generally for funeral whenever a Lodge is showing off on Sundays, or on one of those rare occasions when there is a military band. These Lodges tried to demystify each other as if saying; we are more secretive (or contrary?) than the other Lodges. Shadows remembered one group of well dressed guys marching down the street in a Sunday's funeral procession, each person having green willow leaves in his or her mouth. All the superstitious people were taken back! One can just imagine what impact it had on the hyper superstitious community. Everyone then wonders whom the deceased was worshipping. People want to belong to the Lodges for its social and imaginary economical values. On the other hand they wanted to go to heaven. Now here is the dilemma: how could they enjoy it here and still see the *pearly gates* there!

Apparently, most people then (and even now too) wanted a little more tangible things here, because they joined these Lodges in droves. All the "higglers" with their "partner-throwing" buddies dressed up in their finest for their Sunday evening jaunts towards the cemetery. Shadows remember how impressively they marched, even the older people with their arms swinging away at their sides…marching to the band. It seems funerals were always on Sunday evenings to publicize the Lodges. Could this be just coincidental, or was it planned to exhibit the popularity of these Lodges? Very good management, perhaps we should have an inquest to determine how many of these folks die!

Now the Spirit Healer is still telling her tale, her history…even tales of her early childhood in a nearby village. Shadows remember his childhood and laughed at their similarities. They are indeed people from the same time, of course. It seems in childhood she wanted to go everywhere her older sister went…trying to play the little chaperone with their parents' manipulative consent of course. We all know that generally never stop big sister, as she will send you to the nearest shop to buy "sweety"—sweets. You may run as fast as you can, but whatever they have to do may take a shorter time that your roundtrip… Ask them nine months later! "How could this happens?" Well you wanted date, time, geometric configuration, level of enjoyment. Can you now hear a parent's anguish scream, "No little facie gal, a parent wanted to know about the 'responsibility factor' after the birth…!"

CHAPTER 9

EARLY SCHOOL DAYS (Tulloch)

He too has remembered many childhood tales... seems very silly now but then they were riveting and quite scary too. How about the frightful *Catcher Man* that is supposed to be prowling the school roads? How scary it is for a young child to be aware that everyone else can outrun you because they are all bigger, stronger and faster than you! Yes, the Catcher Man could jump out of his shiny black car and grab you while everyone else runs away! Try dealing with that and sleep soundly at nights knowing that the next day you will again be facing the peril of the "Catcher." Then you got a brilliant idea from an older friend; to walk on the train line. The Catcher Man cannot drive on the railway tracks. All the older guys are telling you that you are too young to walk alone. You finally walked with a strange group of children from another district. They do not talk with you but they are company. You hang back a little distance because someone may pick a fight and you have no help here. They eventually took different paths home, waving loud good-byes to their friends. You are now alone on the tracks with the twilight fast approaching. There is no Black Heart Man or Catcher Man here, but the frightful nightly ghosts and rolling calves stories now comes into prominence...you have to beat the darkness home... You had physically change route to beat the Catcher; presently you now need speed to beat the imaginary ghosts. You start sprinting, stretching out; taking the wooden "pullings" – wooden ties— two, and sometimes three at a time as you observed the flock of birds on the far horizon and those nearby hurrying towards their nest, and then listening to the croaking frogs in the tall grasses along the tracks. You are also being very careful to listen for an infrequent incoming luggage train, or trolley that may creep upon you from behind, and also being very careful not to misstep, or butt your toes. Any of those mishaps could derail your speed and have you tumbling into the darkness, and we all know by now what the darkness brings! You went home panting, *"Mother have you ever seen the Catcher Man or the Black Heart Man?"*

She paused, looking at your sweaty body, up and down before nonchalantly responding, "There is no Catcher Man or Blackheart Man. Is that what you learn in school today?" Well that takes care of that; they never listens to you anyway. Some *"worldy* wise" older guy (about 10 or 12 years old) would come up and say, "Give me piece of your dumpling and I will tell you how to avoid the Catcher Man." "Here." "Want to avoid the Blackheart Man?" "Yes." "Then give me piece of your bulla cake at lunch." Then he tells you whenever you are passing "Dead Man's Bridge," look out for all the black Ford cars. Dead man's Bridge! That "dead" word triggers nightmares galore...! Even now passing Dead Man's bridge one has a tendency to look around at the ever watching hog plum trees across the cane fields ...Oh, what have they done to us during our childhood?

In the morning after you have escaped the Black Heart Man and reached school, then there is *Trevor,* the ultimate school bully that is always lurking someplace. He was well fed, clean and assured. The first observed teacher's pet. Then there was the dangerous *Blacksmith*! Trevor is not in his class. Wiry and self assured but in quite a different physical way from the well regarded Trevor. Blacksmith was not a troublemaker; he was just pure trouble picking on him. He was always "*promping*" (shadow boxing); wearing his old black turtle shell eye glass with the missing left eye lens...perhaps listens to too many Joe Louis boxing tales. In the early phase of the class someone called the monitor a teacher. Another bright girl from the preceding class whispered that she is not a teacher; she is a monitor. The "monitor" pronunciation in patois was interpreted as "man-eater." At least that was what all the first graders heard. She never corrected anyone when they chorused, "Yes man eater!" The children knew the word *man* and the word *eat* so therefore she put those words together and what do you get the teacher, as a man-eater. Just remember they taught us to use syllables, like in the word *to-get-her*! Of all the ghastly European stories about ghosts and witches eating people can anyone guess why the children were so afraid of the teacher? Why not, they had just finished learning about Hansel and Gretel. She was never cruel, but her title was frightening. When she orders sleep breaks all the youngsters tried keeping their eyes open; they want to see if she was about to eat anyone. Bear in mind that the word cannibal was not part of the language then, and if it was the children may have put their pronunciation syllable-spin on it and call it "can- I-bal," meaning "can I bawl"—can I cry, which they were very prone to do in all

97

circumstances. She was always cajoling, "Why don't you close your eyes! Is something wrong?" This is where Trevor the hero comes in. He would always lay on the bench, close his eyes and then quickly opens them to tease the teacher. With that commotion everyone else opens their eyes also, thereby getting a glance of the teacher. She has a strap too, but no one was really afraid of her strap. She never generally uses it except as threats. If she does it was merely symbolic and she could not stand the fake cries. Now that really freaked her out. She would be there hushing for the next hour or so. For the next couple of days she would be giving out special attention to her victim. Most of us possibly got more love from her than at home. It was not very long when the students started associating her with the frightful *Catcher Man*. No one bother to think she is a woman and not a man. Gender to them was not a problem. But why should it be when the conversational term, *"Man a tell you"* is so frequently used to refer to both genders. It was years later when an American woman chided her Jamaican husband for referring to her as *a man* that Shadows becomes more aware of this usage.

Some young students even go so far in saying the caring Monitor was a Black Heart (not Art) man from some other far away village from theirs. They were told that this Black Heart man would remove their heart and put it in a crocus bag. There were no speculations what he was going to do with it. They were all smart enough to know that heart removal would be painful. On the other hand they had possibly never heard of the word art. New words and ideas were scarce then.

During those days some young students acknowledged they came to school just to get the *bulla cakes* at lunchtime. Unknown to them that is how it generally started, until school becomes a part of your life, and you are then hooked in learning things. Lunchtime was always a special time, away from this new and rigid school discipline with strange people called teachers. Some with straps hanging across their shoulders prowling the halls and playground; shouting edicts of conformance…and *"want fi lick you too, and dem a not even yuh mumma."* This was always a sign to give these dangerous *grown ups* a very wide circle. The topics in text books then were quite inconsistent with the culture. What is an "onion and an artichoke" was a frequent question. Then there was "Young Lochinvar" and all the other motivated stories telling us to be brave. The older folks like these stories and relish the idea that their texts were more difficult than the recent "Mother Hen, Mr. Joe…" text book. They failed to see we at least understood what was going on around us, whereas they were still trying to find out "what is an artichoke!" It was so hilarious hearing the villagers decrying the new text book—"A foolishness dem a teach unoo! How can anyone call a goat Mr. Grumps? Calling a goat mister…"

Shadows reminisces on his most frightful trouble at school. It was during lunchtime, while bathing in the river, an older boy jumped on him and he almost suffocated. It seems on this island it was a childhood destiny in having this water problem.

CHAPTER 10

RELIGION

In the towns, Sundays were always quiet with the smell of spicy food (Except for the time when they imported that sickening smelly rice from Rangoon.), and some white American evangelist shouting over the few radios. People soon learn not to pay them "any mind" because the American Blacks were living in misery. And they would never openly discuss any of that. You have to lead by example they say! In his earlier life in another sparsely populated village Shadows is reminded of the reactions to seeing the *first jet plane;* he later read it was a British Hawker Hunter model... But who else, they would never tell you anything about the Americans. It brought panic among the adults. They all looked up in the sky, staring at each other with frightful mask of despair. Shadows now understood their rationale. With their religious Christian background they can only think of one thing: Jesus is coming back for us! Were they prepared, or was it too soon for them? The hanging white exhaust from the jet streams created eerie pictures as if snakes were coming to ambush them among the trees. The supersonic boom created more havoc than the visible plane. They have seen planes before, but not like this. No one knew what it was. There were not many literate persons getting the newspaper anyway. Was this event advertised? Who knows, no one ever reads the news and radio was almost non-existent then? There were no scientific minds here; they were simple village agriculturists who look to the Scriptures for all their experiences when it suited their purposes, of course. This time it did, because anything in the sky was Godly. Good things come from above; bad things are in the earth below. But they eat food and drink water! Of course with the crisis at hand no one would dare rock the boat and point this out to them. No, they were not thinking about sacrificing a little virgin; that would be very unchristian, like those "uncivilized" ones from their ancestor's land. But did that work! Well, if it works who can tell, they may even consider any workable solution to save their own skins, and maintain their priestly "bishop" power base.

There were many little churches, denominations, and other forms of worship... The Seventh Day Adventists and Jehovah's Witnesses were the first friendly Christians he met. All the others seem to be preaching death and human destruction in a fiery lake at Armageddon. Preaching "Repent!" and you have not done anything wrong that you know about. Eventually there comes the Anglican where you could really enjoy yourself without feeling guilty of your innocence...

Recently the feeling among many worshippers are that religion is just another type of entertainment; like Christmas, it has lost its Spiritual significance as people bowed to the glitters of the business world. Shadows overheard a group of people rejecting what one preacher refers to as "African Spirituality." It seems the vocal group prefers just plain Spirituality as opposed to the African-type. The group blamed the African-type for keeping Black people in slavery, and permeated the global feeling that Blacks are the sick chain in the human brotherhood.

Shadows remembered his first verbal contact with a Preacher. He was a quiet man. Later Shadows found out that this man could not read when his grandmother broke ranks and informs him that the pastor was no longer there. That was a real shocker because he had a rousing congregation and was very well respected too. He operates by having the Scripture read to him, and then loudly repeats the messages with emphasis on certain words or sentences. Very neat and quite effective too... Many of his congregants were literate, but that did not stop them from listening to him. Over the years Shadows understood that illiteracy is an obstacle but respect and spirituality are also key ingredients to life. There were numerous spiritual interpretations in this grass root congregation; one of those is where members are always "getting into the spirit." The preacher always has a field day—more like a "feel day" with his sexual sermons. In one incident, a churchwoman decided on having a meeting with a church brother in one of the rooms. It was "determined" that she got "into the spirit" after a "spirit" caught them in the darkened room! The big question was, "What were they doing in there?" The church was in an uproar, quietly making snide remarks, hinting that there seems to be a relationship with the Church Mother and this handsome young male member. The rumors were confusing, because the Mother was not involved in the affairs in the room. Shadows watched the social interplay within the congregation and later theorized the rumor damaged their social cohesiveness. This place was a healing communal home to many; a place where extended families joyfully live. It was definitely a money making affairs, but with a passion for spiritual bidding. They prepared food, drinks, shelter, prayer and guidance to many needy people. Many of the gentries, especially the wives would play the Biblical "Nicodemus-style"—by visiting under the cover of darkness. Of course the police are always trying to plant a spy in the church before the paid healing takes place. The Mother is always finding the spy! An inside job— "a set up!" These worthy "*players*" are no longer with us, and they never did tell before they departed. To soothe your minds, and fixed you steadfastly within your "religious beliefs;" there was this superintendent of police who it is said usually inform... Anyway, most people do not want to hear mystical occurrences, they just want its benefits when it suits them. Later this "place" went into a spiritual tailspin; there were just too many egos. Everyone seems to want the Mother's gift, so numerous pretenders arose after her death. Their onus was not on healing or improved psychic powers on a more profound spiritual pathway. Their desires were pure greed and a better level of social acceptance.

Then there is Shadows favorite deacon from a prominent Baptist church, whom all the children love. He was very nice gentleman, but they claimed he likes his *qq*—quarter-quart of white rum. He was always well dressed and quite informative too with his winning smile. Some congregation claimed he was not in the Spirit, the *spirit* was in him. Another church babble of saying he was always tipsy, and the cane spirit could drive out the real anointed Spirit. Once the minister preached against his drinking habits, then ended the sermon in saying he wished he *could dump all the rum in one big river.* He then asked the deacon to raise a hymn to end the service. The mischievous deacon raise, "By the bank of the beautiful River..." When the pastor rebuked him by telling him rum was his enemy; the deacon responded, "But you say I should love my enemy pastor." The minister replied, "I don't say you are to drink him." "Then lets drink to that then," returned the "spirited" deacon.

In those days, to talk about Africa was to run afoul of the main society, even in the schools. Shadows had quite earlier taken the view that the making of movies like Tarzan was a deceptive move to belittle primitive cultures. Long ago in his pre-adolescence he realized that cheering for the cowboys was the wrong thing to do. The Indians— Native Americans were the heroes. That was when he started reading more books that deal with the issues, and be choosier about the movies he sees. The movie houses were lily white screened. All images of Blacks were as buffoons. They psychologically taught the Black-skinned population to hate themselves and hate and demean each other. Some people would walk out of these movies or refuse seeing them. The majority sees it only as joke and uses it to laugh at their race— that is really denigrating themselves. During the Black American fight for equality there were never any open discussions on that. The farm workers returning never even mentioned events in the South. They were oblivious of that; then again their conditions were no better in Jamaica if they were poor. As a young person the government tightly shut all the avenues for international information exchange among Blacks. Now we wonder if the African's comment that they did not know about the type of slavery practiced in the Western World is true.

Can anyone at this time ever imagine that Marcus Garvey was never discussed in school? Shadows remembers seeing the first photograph of Marcus Garvey on a book in the library. It was not even prominently displayed. The library in Spanish Town placed it on their bottom shelf away from sight. In fairness to them it could be that it was on the G-shelf at the bottom. Then again the only written materials about Blacks were the Ebony magazines exhorting Blacks to solidarity in the USA. Many of the events in that country were so foreign to Jamaicans that they did not see its relevance to them. Then again, numerous people simplistically believed that all the racial problems overseas could be settled by a few "chops" of their cutlasses. The British totally pacifies them by keeping them ignorant on the island. Many of the older Jamaicans believed that Blacks were troublemakers and should be dealt with according to the existing draconian laws. Some openly imputed that "Anywhere Blacks go they are always making trouble!" These older types were too far lost in the British subjugation of their spirit. Herein lies the principle of our parent's giving the authority figures like our teachers the authority to brutalize the young because they are seen as troublemakers. To follow in this sequence is police brutality and then the executioners.

In another remote Village he remembers meeting a man who was not a Christian. There was no religious intolerance towards him. That was a bit of a surprise. But then again, why should it be. The Villagers were not the rabid foam at the mouth type of conservative Church going Christian's zealots, as depicted by the American media for the Southern States. But then Africa was a mysterious place that was never positively spoken of except by the few radical Rastafarians, who had kept the faith after the persecution and prosecution of Marcus Garvey.

Seeing the first non-Christian person who openly disapproved of the Christian religion boggles his young mind. How could anyone not like Jesus the Christ? The confusing part was that the older folks had never troubled him on this point. They still are respectful of this foreign African stranger from where all Black slavery originates. He tells them strange stories of his childhood and is left alone, even protected by them. He childishly wandered around with his utilitarian piece of walking tick. A lost man in a strange religious world... Shadows still wonders what this man's religion was. Was he a Moslem or Animist...he doesn't believe he was Buddhist. No one generally discuss religious issues in these villages. The preachers whenever they come around seem to be always scaring the people about being burnt in hell for their sins. On looking back at those affairs, one cannot say with any degree of certainty it actually makes them any better. It is safer to say it limited their scope of reference, or probably kept them ignorant and utterly confused. There were so many don'ts *"because it is a sin..."* Those were frightful times without any space for fun...the always ever-present explanation, "...because it's a sin and you will burn in hell!" As Shadows grew older and started reading the "West Indian History," he recognized the not too subtle connection with "Slaves obey your masters!" He saw the society with its underpinning of the agricultural working class being comforted by religion. The struggling agricultural workers were always pointing to those in cars passing them while struggling under their heavy burdens; that these upper class people are enjoying their heavens on earth now, because the rich will not go to heaven. The workers took comfort in this idea that they will get their rewards in heaven... Even then Shadows knew this type of reasoning was flawed. When you are carrying a load on your head for miles, and you can have access to a car use it. As there were stringent class distinction coupled with racism, no one was willing to help a struggling sweaty, raggedy, and possibly barefooted working class person by giving them a ride in their car; even if you are taking goods to their home. The contrary problem here was, the Englishman may help you, but the Jamaican white or *brown-skinned* upper class definitely would not ...they were very cruel exclusionists! These were the people that used other people's children as "come around," or "go for;" to climb trees, fetch water and run errands. A kindly Black dressmaker in the village helped a child with clothes, food and medicines. She asked him to pick some limes for her during her illness. The child's mom came running, saying the child had to do an errand for a brown-skinned woman who had never helped her family. Instantly the child rushed to help the brown-woman...*house slaves* never die; they just change their addresses. Is this where we wonder, which is more important knowledge or pigmentation?

A religious friend told Shadows, "When you go to school do not forget GOD!" Shadows was a bit surprised. During that time there were many views that educated people were questioning the religious beliefs. Many schooled people tend to reason more than just react to the pastor's words. It appears that knowledge really is power. Religion is certainly more afraid of educated people. They have a tendency to rock the social order whenever they started thinking for themselves. This saying again brought up the unanswered questions of not being able to positively explain to a child some of nature's simplest things, hence the usual angry response; "You want to fly in the face of God!" Shadows family married into the Pentecostal denomination. This group had helped many people, especially women. Some of the women were badly in need of social directions and a spiritual path. Sometimes to get "on track" one has to bang ones tambourine and rejoice in a mass movement! Some thinker once said; "*...the idea of transcendence is used to obscure oppression.*" The usage of the tactics it seems is to keep the poor and powerless dependent, they are always ineffectually praying for a savior. And Shadows is not talking of the often used 1960s American Civil Right social activist saying "...of wishing for pie in the sky." The religions are noted for trying to erode a person's idea to reason, and then replaced it with some religious doctrine. It seems women are always religious targets to be sequestered, abused or killed by some fake religious person to appease some god. The religious communities all burn 'witches' don't they? Then again there was the other side of women marrying men with aliases. It makes it even more difficult to find them to maintain their family. Most of these marriages were by people trying to play society's little darling. Just try getting a divorce when the marriage was not registered, because the ceremony was performed by an unregistered parson from one of the numerous little "clapped hand" missions. Shadows found out, there were an abundance of these parasites; his friend was a victim. He like the little churches, but he still remembers in his childhood the Spiritual singers, singing, "Let the Power falls on me my Lord, let the power falls on me…" He would look around in awe, stop and ponders the question if powerful falling objects were not dangerous. He did not like the terms "getting into Spirit" and the "Holy Ghost." Can you blame him after the nightly ghostly tales!

Then there were other worshippers. Were they animists? There are always whispers of the "do-good man," the "obeahman," or the "fore-eye man." The latter, Shadows always wonders why so many eyes! He later realized it was not one of arithmetical numbers, but the mystifying ways of dealing with space and time… No, Shadows did not ask a "Fore-eyed" One to define the parametric principles for his name…! Anyway, his friend in later life decided to play around with a married "wrapped-head Revivalist." She asked him never to befriend anyone else then, except her. He played along with her (At least that's what he thinks!) until he decided to marry against her wishes. He was found after three days, hiding in a darkened room without sustenance, weeping and repeating numerous "our father" prayers… He screamed at invisible things for days, and extra days… We can all excuse his behavior by saying he had a mental breakdown, probably resulting in a fear of marriage…? And please, don't ask; I don't know if the family went out to "look for him."

Things have really changed when the penal institutions allowed inmates to come out and give a musical concert. Shadows listens with rapt attention to the Black religious music makers from behind the prison bars who came to entertain the outsiders. All their music has the new dance hall lyrics espousing Christian messages. He marveled how young and spirited they are; very unlike the exhausted barefooted Black Spanish Town prisoners from another era, dressed in short, soiled white pants and shirts, and a ward of His or her Majesty's. The constant it seems that is only the poor Blacks are imprisoned here! Is it that the other races are honest, or perhaps they are too rich to be incarcerated for their transgression? Or possible the black-faced judiciary now still revered the accused "non-Black" skin color? In other words, what is the probability of both a Black person and a non-Black person committing similar crimes, and being convicted with the same sentence? Now it seems things are very different for a nation claiming to be a Christian one, although they kill each other with impunity, and at a reported higher percentile rate than the USA. Statistically it is reported at about 8 times as great! Anyway, the power of forgiveness is divine and comes in various forms. As one mystical preacher said, "The power of the Most High is not limited by time and form."…wishing you well young ones, perhaps never had a chance "to be all you can be;" seeing the system is designed with progressive limits for its poor Black people.

Shadows came out of his reverie thinking how he is always tied to some small village, although he recently sojourns in many large townships. He reasoned he is definitely his mother's son. She always yearns for the rural village life; although during her adolescence she resides in the townships for a while. She finally got it too and it brought contentment to her soul in the latter part of her life. His companion touched his arm and said in her low pitched spiritual tone:

"Come without your rational mind and walk with me in the Spiritual ways you have misguidedly left behind…"

They did not make eye contact, but just quietly laughed together. Their laughter has a bit more warmth than a mere civilize encounter. It is as if they have more personal wishes for this night. She already knew he was enjoying himself. In their last two meetings they had not reached this level of friendship; it was never contemplated then. He is slated to walk with her to another village tomorrow. Shadows started running his mind on different village scenes for this trek. His eyes caught her heaving chest in the darkness, dressed in some of those rural light cotton dresses. She once enlightened him about a man's internal desire for happiness is similar to having,

"A mother's breast, the balm of contentment…"

He had heard many sweet quips before but this one is for the records. She dangles *them* in her summer dress giving that *itchy* feeling that solicits some *comforting* help. He listens with admiration, admiring her gait, buoyancy and rhythm while walking on the narrow road. As he listened to the tone of her voice, watched her heaving bust line she slowly pivoted her head and gazed at him as if reading his thoughts. Her slanted eyes and small sensuous mouth burst into a wide smile. Her translucent eyes were set in a dark face with elevated cheekbones displaying a sensuous small mouth. They both understood something that was beyond word. The next day she mentioned dreaming, or premonitions of future events. He listened to her dreams and remembers that dreams are considered messages from the Cosmos to the soul… She told him of her experience at his family's home…of sensing The Entity by the bed. He invoked a tactful, "Wake me up I want to see (Or is it experienced it too.)" Now he remembers his first early childhood vision of the *"woman"* dressed in white that sat at the foot of the bed while his mother slumbers away in dreamland. She sat there watching him and he stared back at her until his eyes became watery. He then tried drawing the white sheet over his head because he was becoming a bit alarmed. His bedroom was silent and in darkness except for the chinks of light between connecting doors from the other bedroom where his Auntie sleeps with her young baby son. Shadows remembers wanting to awake his mother, but instead went to use the commode very near to the *"woman's"* feet. Now he looks back at it and considers that as an inappropriate move if you are scared. Perhaps he was more afraid of his mother's outburst if he wet the bed, which he never usually does. Shadows told the "big people" in the morning. There were numerous speculations that the "visitor" was his Auntie's husband's mother who was buried in the family plot near by. Years after that he recognized that there are always people seeing ghosts and having ominous dreams...every district has its dreamer!

As the villagers tactfully watched them, Shadows is reminded the cultural nuances of seeing a male-female discussion as an invitation to sex. "*Everything that manifests itself in private has the tendency to give a hint in public!*" He wonders what type of hint they were giving the surrounding inquisitive onlookers. The history he intuitively asked for started to unfold...

He heard her story about economics and the gender counterbalancing act of the society! Who is *right* and who is *otherwise* was not a part of his concerns? He seeks to blame no one; we are all party to the results. He enjoyed walking (or is it roaming) the fields with her. He was shown her birth place, a fruitful minute hamlet off the beaten track. He conversed with her Indian friend, and got some good views about the safety of their neighborhood. They impressed him with their cooperation as a village unit. The village safety was dependent on a vigilant neighborhood watch, "beware thieves and rapists!" It was frightening, but here they have the "dead statistics" to prove they are serious about a crime free neighborhood. The community has the most impressive group of children he has ever seen at a village Basic School. Shadows observed children at play, climbing tress, shouting and laughing in their little groups. Then there was this little rude boy with the most atrocious cussing language. Shadows was instantly reminded of the word he had said to his brother one Sunday evening while they were at play; although his language was never like the sentences this infant was stringing together. That was a fateful Sunday for him. His brother, the dutiful and obedient religious type shouted his question so his mom heard it. She calmly asked how that question came up. Of course his "Mr. Do Gooder" brother told the truth. She lapsed into her calm Sunday's voice and informed him "...we will discuss this when you return from playing..." Big threat! He agonized over his punishment for weeks, but she never mentioned it again. Later he realized why; parents were unable to have sexual discussions with children. You just may have to use names that they did not want to hear coming from you. Everything then was glossed over and sanitized...as a white plaster covering a festered sore.

CHAPTER 11

REFLECTIONS continues...

He is observing this entire event and remembering his Village during his formative years. He recalled his childhood hero, "Backra," the slingshot warrior who could shoot what he called a "babble dove" and many more big wild birds. He also remembers Backra's brother, Budhai whose name was always pronounced as "Bud-eye." Then his other friend Herman who gave him the Mysore cow's story of how the cow uses its tail to cover you with its mess if you should walked through the pasture, and climb a tree to escape it. You would scratch yourself then fall to sudden death on its horns...

Most Villagers then smoke cigars made from tobacco leaf. Ready-made cigars were too expensive. The big greeting was, "How strong is your tobacco!" People were always sampling each other tobacco and rating its strength. There was a definite search for stronger tobacco. It seems throughout history that people always wanted stronger dope! The word dope was never used then. Cigarettes were only for the upper groups or the trendy city folks, or for some of those who buy the daily newspaper each morning. These village "newspaper readers" were the respectful information gurus. They were generally dressed in khaki suits and Busha hats—safari-type hats, wearing clean, shiny shoes that were the status symbols of emulating the British safari type dress. They have information and were willing to get more information. Some of these folks were illiterate, but they would tactfully ask someone to read them the news. This now brings into context the present day situation where numerous island Black persons, mostly poor women are caught going overseas with their stomachs (or other places) filled with contraband. Can they read, or have they not heard the news coming out of the industrial *global villages* that there is a "wideband" technology that is very effective against these types of trading? It seems the old attitude of not passing on information to our offspring, coupled with the new intense "global village" greed is finally wreaking havoc with these new-aged uninformed "mules" with their numerous little children waiting hopelessly at home. Shadows is not being a warped conservative by expecting some inestimable purity of social values, but neither he cannot be expected to be some naive social apologists continually blaming the government and its policies for these individuals childish and foolish actions.

The other agricultural working class was dressed in blue jean materials called "old iron blue." Shoes were optional. It should be emphasize that many people walked barefooted or wear board slippers. The strange thing is they would rather wear the silly "clippity-cloppity" board-slippers, rather than wear a more effective "power slippers"—the fore runner of the trendy '60s "Jesus boots" made out of rubber tire. The Rastafarians with their radical message of Black awareness were the only makers of power slippers. The slippers were black color. Imagine a bearded Black man *uttering* (The Rastas then like using the word *utter* for its Biblical impact.) "Black Power-slippers!" Get it;

Black Power? That was long before the upheaval in Mexico City with the radical black gloved Black Power salute from the noble Black American Olympians. Yes, the Jahs then were just too radical for the docile, class conscious, pale-pigmented-adoring Black masses. There was always a constant thirst for knowledge in these villages. News was at a premium. It was in this context that Miss Agnes the neighborly ganja dealer kept abreast of the changing events. Young Shadows grew up with her son, "Boy." No naming surprise there; her daughter's name was "Gal-Gal." There will be no silly joke here like, "*check their genders and named them so, lest we forgot who they are when we clothed them,*" about a kind and gracious neighbor. He later found out that her son Boy and he accompanied her in buying the *stuff* one night. He had no idea where they went; he was too glad for the trip away from home.

The whole ganja secrecy started to unravel when a new carefree younger villager came on the scene. He stupidly asked Shadows to buy some *tobacco* from Miss Agnes! Shadows told him that Miss Agnes did not sell tobacco. The foolish younger man insisted that Miss Agnes sells *funny tobacco,* and young Shadows were to ask her to "*trust*" him some. The innocent young Shadows continually telling him he was wrong, because the tobacco seller was Miss O'Connor. The silly man finally wised up and recognized his mistake. His hasty agreement to his mistake and his panicky urging Shadows to quickly go home and say nothing to anyone rings an alarm bell. When Shadows told his mother about the incident she screamed, panicked and almost spill the dinner she was preparing in the kitchen. She was so agitated; her demeanor gave away the play. She opened her eyes with a commanding scream: "You stay there!" She hastily ran to Miss Agnes, almost jumping the green orilla fence, complaining in hushed tones about the new resident… When his mother stated "Me and that man *no plant gungo a line,*" his child's literal mind starts wondering about planting. The statement was not too conceptual. He saw a "morning work"—cooperative farming— where food is provided during planting seasons, but that "would be buyer" was not there, neither is he a neighbor. Miss Agnes instantly wrapped her head in a very bright color cloth, took her belly-woman cutlass, and assertively strides down the track in rage, muttering: "*A hawk and patto race wid mi and him today. Hmm…him a go mek mi have him up in a mi stomach now!*" Now the puss was definitely out of the bag. Shadows had never seen ganja, and had never heard much about it but he knew something serious was happening. He knew his loving neighbor; this kind woman he grew up with whom was always sending his dinner and sometimes breakfast over the fence was a *ganja seller*. **Miss Agnes** returns quickly and started rearranging her house. There was a high level of watchfulness after that. The new neighbor was severely reprimanded by all concern. After all that it still took years for Shadows to recognize that a certain man who was always smoking in the dark, outside Miss Agnes' home was actually a user. No wonder he was always so laid back when he was driving the children to school in his cart. Perhaps smoking was his only entertainment because there were no other forms of amusement around except telling Anancy and ghost stories during the nights, and perhaps guessing the answer to cultural riddles.

"Riddle me this, riddle me that. Guess me this riddle and perhaps not… Chip cherry bears cedar!" Well, yes, a lot of that too…

Shadows recalled the time they had a young visitor name Joslyn. That night his mother told them a special Anancy story. She ended the tale with the phrase, "Jack Mandora, me no choose none." He asked her for the meaning, and she told him that they always ended the Anancy stories with that phrase because she did not make up the story she just tells it. He could not make sense out of the phrase. He just could not see the relevance. Immediately their little visitor, more an interloper, interferes saying, "Is true that is the way the story always ends!" His mother laughed and gave her approval. Shadows tried getting more information, but he knew she was not about to say anything else. She just rubbed Joslyn's head and went to her room. That was the beginning of a ticklish relationship with him…Shadows rememebers Joslyn, as a motherless project who one day just appears without warning. Joslyn starts ingratiating himself to Shadows' mother. It appears she was the first person to show him any sign of love. Joslyn was in a very bad physical shape, but his mind was keen. He was intellectually sharp for a young child. The neighbor, Mrs. Tucker, confounded the situation more by accusing Shadows of peppering Joslyn's eyes. At this time Shadows had no idea that the accusation was actually directed at his mom who came from another district. She was being picked on. Mrs. Tucker knew Joslyn's mother, but had refused him refuge. This was the same woman that Shadows caught "raiding" his mother's flowers. She acted so guilty, in trying to cut the flowers as quickly as possible, and in silence too. He silently came out of the house asking, "What are you doing?" Her curt reply was, "Shut up!" Shadows replied, in a very out of character, "Thief." You were never allowed to address any "Big People' in this manner. She made no effort to reply. Her priority seems getting away from the flower garden. She hastily did so. Unknown to Mrs. Tucker, his mother was in earshot of her cruel lie. It infuriates her hearing this woman referring to Shadows as. "...that little boy is like a murderer...he hold Joslyn and peppered his eyes..." Shadows eventually visited her home as an older boy. It seems his mom had never felt real comfortable with the Tuckers after that. They never visited each other. It finally came out that Shadows father was expected to marry her daughter! Everyone has secrets in these villages. Little Joslyn was not one of those adoptions without "papers" that were prevalent during those times when the parents would later showed up when the child could be of service as their go-for! All the light-skinned people wanted to "adopt" children, especially those of darker skins to be their virtual slaves with no response from a cold and indifferent community ...no one cares. They would whisper about a child's condition but there would be no action on their part. There were no Child Rights; a child just exists on sympathy...like the Black race co-exists on other races' sympathy. There is no strong country capable of standing up for their Rights!

He had a few distasteful boyhood encounters with little Joslyn. He remembers the "goat moving" incident. Where the Dragon Blood plants silhouetted against the background of the diminishing twilight was a quick stepping manlike figure comes striding on the narrow, partially plant covered pathway. The darkness converged on his raggedy working clothes giving this eerie picture of a gaunt, rambling figure with what appears as a long dangling cutlass in his left hand. They both remember a man had recently died in the village, and now they equate the approaching figure as the ghosts of the departed. They fought viciously to be the first to climb over a wooden gate that separates them from the main path. Shadows held onto the agile Joslyn who would have quickly leaped over the gate. A fight ensued as the nimble Joslyn tries to be the first to climb over the gate. The briskly walking "ghost" closed the distance between the fighting boys, the darkness became more intense. The blackbird made its last sound for the day as the boys screamed with anger and frustration to put a safer distance between themselves and the frightfully onrushing visitor. They looked down the path in the onrushing darkness and see the striding shape with waving limbs like tentacles and opened soundless mouth pointing at them, as if fiercely threatening them.

They screamed as the vegetation nightlife came to life with the chirping of the numerous crickets, and bugs welcoming the last rays of the setting sun. The new environmental sound startled the boys into a screaming frenzy. They quickly look for other enemies among the darkened vegetation. Immediately an urgent voice from the increasing darkness chided them, "Bwoy unoo see how unoo would kill unoo self through foolishness!" The temperamental tethered goat strained against their short tangled ropes in the darkness as they intensified their efforts to go home, bleats, "Mayaa!" as if in agreement with the stranger. The boys stopped and quickly ran towards the goats. They pleaded with their still unrecognized, but newfound human friend to stay awhile while they quickly try loosening the goats before he leaves them alone in the increasing darkness. The stranger refused, but compromised by telling them they should work quickly before he goes through the gate. He immediately slowed his pace to accommodate them. They loosen the goats and scampered away home... This stranger has never been seen in the village before. Or after that! Where did he come from? Over the years Shadows always wonder who he was.

In those days, social manners were very important. A child was under the scrutiny of the society, especially so in the rural areas. To screw up was a poor reflection on your parents and the rest of family. How many times were you to listen to your uncles and grandparents saying, "None of our family ever do things like that, it is only *worthless people* do things like that!" This type of talking is not just idle chatter; it is a threat to you the young ones. Take it seriously or bear the consequences if you ever caused the *others* to label your family as those *worthless people*. Parents are always threatening children with dire consequences if you play around with their social history. It was in this strict condition that Shadows and his then archenemy Joslyn participated in Shadows' first social community gathering at an in-laws' wedding. They sat to eat and Joslyn kept watching him, beating him to every choice morsel. At the last piece of meat on their common plate, Shadows got tempted and quickly shoved the meat in his mouth. He was taking no chance of losing it. Joslyn went home and complained how Shadows had rudely behaved. He made it seems that Shadows ate the food ravenously and caused shame on the family. There were concerns about his disrespectful behavior. The discussion went far back into the night. He was being interrogated by his parents to determine if they had any cause to fear social repercussions. Joslyn was in fine conspiratorial mettle when the numerous questions were asked:

"Did anyone say anything about your behavior? What did Mrs. Mutty say? Did she see you? Did you choke? Did you belch around the table? Did you beg anything…? Did Mrs. Mutty talk to anyone about you? Did… etc?"

Mrs. Mutty was the local *labrisher*— newsmonger. She was from a big family and has friends in numerous adjoining districts. She was like the local *newscaster* and would consistently *stained* other families with her indelible *labrish* brush. Shadows remember his mother's nostrils were opened, and her chest was heaving in the dim yellowish lamp light. She was outwardly calm but definitely disturbed. Shadows recalls how he wanted to sleep so badly. He stopped defending himself and lapsed into a sleepy silence. Joslyn went prattling on until the "big people" turned the table on him by telling him that they will not allow him to go out again with Shadows, because of Shadows' bad influence on him. He immediately did a subtle change and become a little kinder with his story. It seems Shadows' story was not colorful enough for the critical family audience as that of the lying Joslyn.

On looking back on the incident, perhaps there were no merits to Joslyn's complain…there were some choice morsels or drink that Shadows believes should be his; seeing that *de ole lyad boy* was racing to eat every choice morsel. Shadows remembered being mildly surprise when he heard Joslyn was not coming back home. It was the first case of indifference he experienced. Joslyn was considered the enemy in all its notorious phases. It was funny that Shadows always expects meeting Joslyn again. He still wonders what happens to him, especially when he heard that he is now a preacher. Shadows' mother went to her grave praising little Joslyn and his willingness to help. The years had passed, and now the Joslyn's saga is just a mere childhood memory. Now Shadows wonders if Joslyn was all that bad, or it was pure childish jealousy… to Joslyn's credit he was very intelligent, especially so for his age. He knew he had a good thing going with the family, and he used it to his advantage too. He had to, or he would possibly perish. If there were no one to look after the little children, then the poor things will have to do something for him or herself…obeying the primal command to save their lives. Shadows is still mystified by this competitive little child, and still wonders who was older. He knew that the competitive Little Joslyn did just what he had to do to survive. Live on Joslyn…!

In those days the social attitude towards begging was very plain. You just do not beg, even if you were a child. Hankering or just pure "henka" is one of those transgressions that could bring banishment to another family member, or worse punishable with having the *henka*-dog's nickname. How about, "Come here

"Missa Henka-dog!" There was no political correctness then. Many parents bruised their children's ego and helped giving them low self-esteem. There was a strong social policy then of not eating from others. Every parent has his or her approved list. Of course they did not openly tell you not to eat from an individual; a child may tells that someone and get your parents in trouble. (Children were never socially trusted.) It works like this if someone gives you food; your parents would request that you take it home and sit and eat it. Hence do not eat on the road. With this in mind most people would not want to give you the food to take home. Your parent may know what they had for dinner and then criticized it. These people were fiercely private. If you take it home your parent would have asked who gave it to you. You have to tell them. Of course they are going to ask why it was given to you. This is asking if you asked for it, or were *henka-in* around their table. In this case they may decide whether you should have your dinner, and or take the gift-food away. They may tell you that whenever a specific person offers you food to tell them that you are not hungry. You instantly know that you should not eat from this person. The big hypocritical problem is whenever you are visiting this person with your parents, and you are offered food before your parent can say, "He already ate; his belly is full!" When you refused the donor will say, "You think I am unclean? You mother (never your father.) tells you not to eat from me?" At that time expect a stare from the donor, which means "You hear say I am an *evil-dabbler*!" Now expect your hypocritical smiling parents to perk up, "Why you don't want Miss Loris' food? I never tell you not to eat from her." Right! She really had never told you so. So you *forced* the food in silence while the "big people" chitchats, knowing very well that they have just sold you out to maintain social harmony. On the way home they are very sensitive, and have only good things to say about Miss Loris while *in your earshot*. Of course you have nothing to say. No body ever asked you for your opinion anyway... But one thing you still know; do not ever eat from Miss Loris whenever they are not there.

Whereas Joslyn was considered an enemy, Shadows natural brother was aloof. His brother started reading at an early age, and therefore leap-frogged into some intellectual space where childhood is bypassed. His brother reads and listens to too many nightly Bible verses. In the morning it is the newspaper or some book without pictures. He is always reading something, and then everything he finds. He never plays. Shadows remember being so upset that he called him a harlot. No one ever tells what a harlot was. Shadows knew it was something bad. His elder brother just laughed and replied that he was not a woman. That was puzzling, but no other question was asked. He wondered if the Bible was such a good book, then how comes so much bad things, like harlots were in it. It seems whenever anyone reads the Bible it was always about an angel with a fiery drawn sword and people talking about some scary lightening and thunder, fire, Revelation, Armageddon and something they called brimstone. It seems if you are not righteous then God will just kill you. Every explanation is with religious overtones or ghostly interactions. In other words God the Father is destructive, and we are just actors in this life; seizing the moment. Reading the Bible were always about death and destruction, and the crucifixion of the good one they called Jesus Christ who was kind. Later they threw in a new wrinkle called the Holy Ghost! Shadows recalled his spiritual recoil, and long pause while silently gazing in the distance when he heard that name from his nightly hymn-singing, pig-feed-cooking, older friend Herman. Herman said the word "ghost," this time a new ghostly name emerged, the Holy Ghost. Now that was scary when taken into a religious context. All ghosts he thinks was in their graves some places not mixed up with the heavenly bodies. It should be noted at that time that the words spirit and ghosts were synonymous with fear. There definitely was no fun whenever the Bible is read. Then there was David the shepherd. But what was a sheep. He has never seen any sheep. Cows, yes! But sheep and shepherds never... There were numerous door to door Seventh Day Adventists and Jehovah Witnesses that were quite presentable and friendly. Many people it seems tried to avoid the Jehovah Witnesses. These two religions were more conversationally acceptable than the blood and thunder Baptist preachers were. Shadows think they actually scare people away from the Christian religion in the early days. Everything to them was a sin punishable by brimstone and fire...a young mind finds it difficult to grow under such stressful limitation. Then again the centrist churches were asking people to dress in a way one could not afford. It seems the idea was to build a social registry society, not a spiritual one.

In Shadows quest to count and read, it seems his brother was unwilling to help him. His older brother was the main competition, and Shadows definitely was not a competitive factor there. The man was in another realm somewhere far above him. Like their father he was sharp. After a while Shadows was considered as a family throwback or possible a nonentity. He remembers his father took out a huge piece of carpenter's chalk and gave him a test when his mother was absent. He could hardly help himself in deciphering the letters or words. His father finally laughed, and comforted him with some food and drinks saying, "How come she says you can read!" Shadows knew his father was actually laughing at his mother, not at him. His father believes he won the game because the son he paid much attention was excellent. The big thing then was counting to a hundred. He remembers reaching ninety-nine and then rationalized his counting by saying *ten-ty*, ten-ty one…then *eleven-ty* because ten and eleven were the following counting series numbers after nine. His brother sat there through all this nonsense and never once corrected him…just muttering "*stooge on the loose.*" After about three weeks his brother was reading his newspaper and finally got disgusted and said, "It is not *ten-ty* it is *one hundred*." He was laughing too. Shadows wonders if his loving brother thought he was joking all those weeks in counting, ten-ty one, ten-ty two… The defeating thing is he wanted to learn to count, but would not have done it around the one person who was most willing to help him, his mother. She would eventually ends the session with his punishment by giving him a test…that was no fun ending. Punishment has its place as a deterrent, but so many times it seems as just a hindrance to progress.

His brother was just too laid back at times. He recalls seeing the rainbow at Natural Bridge… such is generally seen way up in the sky on the far horizon. And no one he knows knew any physics for its explanation. Everyone will tell you about the first rainbow as the Biblical symbol as the Creator promised never again to destroy the earth with water. The ROYGBIV (Red- Orange-Yellow-Green-Blue-Indigo-Violet) color acronym was never mentioned. As Shadows walked around the dimly lit rocks there stood before him a dynamic burst of shimmering color, an actual rainbow in all its glory arching towards the strong glare of sunlight…twinkling in the misty spray of the splashing water trickling from off the rocky morass surfaces… His young heart skipped a beat as he remained momentarily transfixed in watching the rotating misty water particles being moved by gravity and the wind…falling to the ground as the bright slanting sunrays enlivened the musky catacombs. It stood there before him, damp and vibrating as if alive in its swirling rainbow colors; with its misty, dark handle scythe-blade shaped pattern as if watching him, studying him before it makes its next move… The pervading swooshing water sound under the bridge overpowers his senses, locking him into a world of awe, intermingled with his fear. He knew nothing then about the grim Reaper's scythe as a sign of death, because the question of life or death was not a puzzling one. He knew he could only choose life, because death then was a blurred question mark, just an imaginary point, somewhere, very far down life's winding roadway. He realized he was dizzy…he was holding his breath too long. For stability, he cautiously dug his now shriveled and hawk-like fingers into the dampened morass and rocky cleft, which seems his only solace and natural link with reality, and to his hold on life. He ponders the enigma in front of him, wishing it would go away...He dare not touch; a thought that never crossed his mind. The only thought was the getting away from this unexplainable phenomenon and return to his older brother's company. He slowly and carefully stepped backwards on the cold slippery rocks, now too afraid to turn his back on this strange thing that continues to mesmerize his senses. In the safety of the separating rock he looked at his brother and pointed... His brother saw his face and calmly mentioned, "You saw the rainbow." At that moment Shadows did not know if he likes his brother or detests him. Not with a childish dislike, but with a deep sense of spite. He was his only brother, the one young person he really likes as a family...he should have warned him! Instead he sat there splashing in the cold water and acted as if nothing disturbing had just happened to his brother... But looking back now, that was his brother's chief characteristics; he was always unruffled in the face of adversity. Shadows recalls their last togetherness episode of newspaper reading in the *big city*. Yes, he finally made it to the Big City to see the places he had read about so many times. During their childhood his brother always talked about the buses and trains going to the City. He knew all the railway stations' names and distances apart, but he had never been there except Riversdale and probably Troja. He was like their loving Auntie, a city lover where the action is. At a tender age he understood the government of the country, and who was who under the British Colonial system. Shadows still remembers them reading the newspaper together that last evening. It was the last thing they did together... It was a heart-rending event, especially so soon after their mother's death but life goes on... Again it was another sad message after school! Perhaps not going to school or more like not coming from school could have saved him numerous emotional twists...just a thought. Choices!

On the other side he reflects on the event with his brother in the hills while gathering firewood and digging for yams for the nightly "cook out" with the hog feeding cookers. For a very short while, the place was rife with an iodoform smell, a very prevalent medicine during that era. People generally had so many nicks and bruises, a legacy of their marginal agricultural life styles. An iodoform smells always triggers one of those many ghost stories. He looked around and saw or imagined he saw a dark barefooted apparition, with rolled up cuffed *old iron blue* pants, rolled up below the knees and smoking a tobacco pipe. It seems there were numerous sightings of similar apparition in those days. Anyway, fertile mind or not that is against the point...This *appearance* called for a quick escape. He dangerously launched an escape by leapfrogging over his elder brother. Unfortunately for him he ran in the wrong direction towards an area where there were graves. He met his in-laws hustling towards home with some dubious tales of ghosts sighting also. His young in-laws were never known for speaking the truths. They too listened to too many ghost stories while cooking hog feedings during the nights. The elder brother was a real scary tale weaver, but his younger brother, Sprinkler Joe was the prime mover for all the nightly tales. How can he ever dismiss the incident with Sprinkler Joe? He postulated that ghosts did not like bad words, so this gave him an excuse to use indecent words. His excuse *I was saving my life from the Jumbi...* One night when all *the big people* were absent a *shape* came outside the house and began poking a white stick through the door. Joe began using some of the most profane languages imaginable. Making matter worst he solicited everyone in the group to help him use these languages in the most vociferous way. He reasoned that a more magnified response would thwart the ghosts. A very reasonable assumption, but the intruder was his loving uncle trying to frighten us. Joe was just lucky his parents did not come home and hear them. Sometimes Shadows laughed, thinking that he should have shouted with them as good friends would, but he never believe it was a ghost trying to hurt them. At times one has to follow ones own interpretation and leave the herd mentality alone...

CHAPTER 12

"MUMMAW"

Years have passed and now he recollects watching The Old One sipping a beer with relish. It was warm outside with a slight wind that would have rustled the window curtains. But no night breeze would be admitted through an open window here. The culture taught the night air brings sickness. Night was a time of ghostly delights for the outsides. The huge room was dim and quite habitable. There was life all around it, very young lives too. Unbelievable, but some were even sleeping beneath white sheets! The Old One sipped her icy cold beer between moans of contentment. She gave a graceful belch then ponders the level of righteousness of imbibing spirits at her advanced age when she was on the road to meet the angel Gabriel at the pearly gates... Her question was deflected by a joke that if she believes, "One spirit drives out the other." The Old One was momentarily quiet, but later advised that anyone over forty should watch what they eat and should not eat pork. She was a pork lover in her younger days. She was a rabid political animal who took the view that a certain weak minded politician in a leadership position from her party was a plant from the other party. She likes intense political discussions and was good at it too. She watched the development of Adult Suffrage on the island and made some very astute observations about the demise of some of the leaders. The family females always agree with her until Shadows who was then considered the young male rebel opposed her in their numerous heated discussions. Shadows' Auntie had asked that he takes a less adversarial approach during these discussions. The Old One got quite upset at their next discussion. She wanted to know if he was a "fool like the other foolish set of *piss-pots* who live in this yard!" This was indeed a very strong negative description for her compliant family members. It was obvious she likes the political arguments. Her voice almost screaming, with her acrid comment: "Send you to school to learn, now you come back agreeing with everything me say…like a slave …Foolishness!" The Auntie again requested a change in tactics to the former heated arguments. Shadows obediently returned to the old politically charged situation; it was just fine with the Old Matriarch, a fight with equal respect.

Shadows watched the older woman, his grandmother, and remembered the funeral of her oldest daughter, his mother. He recalled her silently slipping away to a secluded spot under a large star-apple tree; tied her belly and silently wept. He was weeping too, but less openly. It seems they both needed privacy to console their grief. It was as if both had been summoned by a Higher Power to this one common spot, to terminate the rift between the spirit of her recently departed daughter and a sorrowful mother.

He has since became more matured, and recognized this is the mother of the woman who took him miles on her back and shoulders when he was a sick child to the only available medical clinic. He certainly got all the available medicine from those big and dreadful "slavery-time" hypodermic needles!

Everything in those days that were big and odious was referred to as "slavery time!" Very conceptual! The transportation then was limited to walking, taking the train in one direction in the morning or evening, or taking a bus... No other mode of transportation was then available to them. That action was love; it could not have been anything otherwise, because the other mothers from his neighborhood with their sick children had never made the effort. It seems the majority of them just did not find it necessary. Or their children were not a high priority. There were numerous sicknesses and few cures for: yaws, jiggers, sore toes, malaria (No, dengue fever comes later.) He recalled screams in the mornings coming from his next door neighbor, an older boy with a sore toe. The usual medicines were iodoform dressings, bushes, or copper-stone...Shadows reached across time to smile at his mother: he remembers as a sick child he could do any sick thing except vomiting, or as she called it "throw up." She had this very insane dislike for that action. She would get ballistic and downright upset. He remembered eating the cassava dish and retching in his sleep...that really got her attention! There was no scream then; it was a different game of silence and care, punctuated by whimpering and heavy breathing sounds... Perhaps she thought that was the end. This was a tragic time for the community because a loving family had a few of their younger children wiped out by the dreadful *ackee* poisoning.

In a fit of rage and despair Shadows remembered asking his grandmother how come she is now weeping, if it was for joy. She just looked at him in silence with teary brown eyes. Such beautiful brown eyes; showing a tinge of blue that he had never before seen. He had no idea she was that beautiful. Shadows remembered staring at her with defiance and with no level of love or respect. He stared at her as if he was in control. His grandmother stared back in silence with the streaming tears running down her old brownish cheeks. She was beautiful! She now seems much prettier than his mother does too. He had never seen her beautiful grayish–brown eyes before. Both mother and daughter had never got along well in life, but now here she sits on the ground weeping uncontrollably. He remembered his mother's discussions depicting this woman as being uncaring to her. He also remembered this woman's mildly slapping him for putting a pea up his nose…after she and others had trouble removing the pea. He had never been slapped by anyone else. Perhaps she saved his life for he could hardly breathe then… He remember this woman for not giving the same respect and attention she gave her granddaughters during the few times they had meals together. She definitely was not his favorite person. He had never seen any kindness from her. To him she was a virtual stranger with a grandmother's name and level of higher respect. As he watched the grand old lady enjoying the beer he knew they loved each other. He smiles contentedly reflecting on her last effort to mold him into something he could never be happy with. She wanted him to act on stage…he tried *muffing* it but she still wanted him to try out… How could he; he had laughed at his friends playing in the school cantata…"Born a King on Bethlehem's plain…" So how could he now allow this to happen to him! She finally gave up. Looking back now, it could have been a good thing, and it probably would have made her happy. Childhood days are so rife with confusions. Over the years she had been his everything, as a total reversal from the efforts given to his mother. He is so happy with her... He had never vocally apologized for his childish effort of reprimanding her; but the vibrations of the heart have its spirited apology. As his dear Auntie said during prayer on her deathbed, "We pray for everything we have said and do, and also for those things, which are within our heart that we haven't said."

He knew his grandmother is very unlike her sister, the delightfully rude and vibrant grandaunt who is capable of discussing anything. He remembered her openly asking him if he was having an affair: "Cus-cuss are you using that thing yet?" "Lawd sister you are going to dead and go to hell!" shouted his alarmed grandmother reaching for her sister's biggest Bible. Please don't ask if the bible size makes a difference. Perhaps it had bigger print to help the older eyes to see with more clarity. Anyway, grandmother could not believe her elder sister would dare ask her studious grandson that brazen question. The old grandaunt roared with laughter, and chided her sister that she was always foolish and too afraid. An evaluation that was more accurate than first believed, but we are what we are and love makes it easier, said someone so long ago...Amen. The old grandaunt remembers the restriction the society and her crass and brutal husband placed on her before she bolted to her brother for refuge. She enjoyed a freedom devoid of males in her older days...but one that embraces freedom of speech, worshipping and stable economics. A spiritual freedom that enriches the soul... An old church friend once told his grandaunt she was going to find a perfect man again and get married. The elegant Old Feminist hawk, lit her chalk pipe, stared in the distance before telling the friend that she too had found her perfect brown-skinned man, but he told her that he too was looking for the perfect woman so he couldn't marry her! She then removed the unlit pipe from her mouth, stared at her friend and laughed. The youthful Shadows at that time did not understand her comment. Years later after her death he understood: do your search but first know yourself and define who you are...make certain that you are perfect before looking for perfection because perfection in itself may be looking for perfection too.

On reflecting on these events Shadows agrees that a child really never understands the emotions between a mother and a daughter. The female are generally the bedrock of the family, especially when so many males are prone to play the active *sperm donors role.* One old preacher excused was that a man by nature is generally more interested in his wife than his children; whereas the wife is more interested in the children's welfare than her husband. We will not get too psychological here and ask why the man is so interested in the woman at the expense of his children. His mother spent many years asking him never to be one of those uncaring men. He has obeyed her and also his conscience. Her asking was more like a *feminist's tongue-lashing.* "I would rather see your grave than bringing you here to make children suffer!" Shadows now realized that she believed she would be liable for the karmic blame if her son ever went that careless route... This cannot be said about his cousin, the

"Breeder," his grandaunt's nephew. He is one of those donor types, believing he is a "selective breeder" on someone's slave farm. The unfortunate thing is there were numerous women who believed he was! He was so different from his grandmother and the rest of her family. He was a regular *"maid man,"*— always romancing the maids and with dire consequences. He was considered a very bad person; without honor so was brutally shunned by the family. Sometimes when Shadows remembers him he equated his behavior to the slaves used to rape and breed stocks in the slaver's castles in Ghana. Integrity where women were concern was never his forte. The greatest joke is he fell in love, in real love and married with two beautiful daughters. His best friend eventually took away his wife. What a piece of convoluted justice after all those years of philandering. The "Breeder" was so devious that when a woman seeks child support; he would befriend her and then have another baby. During that time he would not be paying support. Shadows remembers asking him if it was cheaper by the dozens. On one occasion he became upset when he believes Shadows took away the church girl he wished to marry when he went looking for work in the tourist area. Church people then had the tendency of ostracizing pregnant unmarried women. Where is the love? Later, he returns berating Shadows, saying that Shadows allowed a strange man to come in and take away his woman, and get her pregnant. That conversation was a warning that simple adolescent "relationships" can result into life's future nightmares! He learnt then to always asks the right question, and don't quickly voice your conclusions. When timely asking the correct question;

there is a high probability of receiving a truthful reply. Men within the society then, had to be very careful because their female relatives were prone to agree with a mother claiming her child is yours. Those were not the days of the biotech revolution where genetic evaluation could be used to ascertain relationships. A woman's word was the only truth…and the judges would definitely agree with her with their usual dreadful decision: "Adopt it!" This decision was generally never too effective because many men just runaway. Others compromised with the woman and made more babies, thereby compounding the problem. At that time going to jail was never an option. Doing that would socially scar you and your family for life… "They have a prison bud boy in their family!"

YOUNGER RELATIVES

During those days when the coming generation was growing up, his grandmother was the one who always stay at home. She always has the younger ones sitting on a long bench, and feed them goodies. Shadows eventually named the bench, the Mampala Bench. The young males under Grandma's protective wing had comical names like "Long Tolly Woppy"—don't ask why, "Nan," a mystic who *know-eth* all things, "Turtle" for his good rounded vibes… Then the girls were called "Juddy-drownded." Just don't call her that because she would cry going into the next century. Juliet the tall fiery frown-faced one with a nice voice, who was always frowning as if articulating, "Who do I slap next, damn it!" By this time the place was bubbling with all types of family drama. The younger girls were trying to "strut their stuff" with various interplays within the Church groups. Prior to this era the mystifying Rock and Tawny dropped a bombshell by telling off one of the pastors who called her mad, "Lord this one really is mad!" Can you imagine a church member's daughter in good standing replying, "A who you think you *expletive* talking to; you...." The Auntie returned home dumbfounded, silent and quite chastened. She went straight to her room and neither mother, nor daughter ever mentioned the incident for years. At this time there emerged a tussle between rigid old values versus new values on sexual interpretations. In this cauldron comes a young cousin, Juggu, the young radical social orders disturber, and Cecil the newly respectful young man on the bloc. Ode to a fallen family hero...sometimes it is not the very brilliant mind that does well in this world, it is the disciplined mind with the drive to persist. Shadows can still hear his Auntie questioning, more like giving the parental ridicule that etched the name "Juggu" to her young high spirited daughter. "Are you some *juggu-bup bala-hoo*, slippers drawing market gal why you won't behave yourself...and talk quietly like a young lady!" In those days you have to be careful of parent's whenever they start looking askance at you during a conversation. After that everyone started calling her "Juggu," even her mom did. We all believed it was more appropriate than her pet name of Queenie. The name change was years after Shadows met her for the first time as a small girl. When Shadows inquired what was her name the child ran away around the house hiding, and saying, "My name is Teen-ige." Of course

141

this is a place where everyone has a pet name, and no one is actually registered as a Queenie. (At least we hope so!) He stood there pondering the name of his beautiful little cousin. He smiled and again asked for clarity on this troublesome name. She repeated the same name. Eventually some of her solder sisters cleared up the pronunciation. He understood the reasoning behind the Queenie name. If the visiting monarch is a queen then you may choose to name your child a "queenie" to commemorate the visit. This is saying she was born in the year of the Queen's visit to the island. Now here is the curve, the darn Queen comes back a few more times and perhaps now you need a number to remember which visit it is. The versatile Auntie asked Shadows if one is a number. They both laughed and the Auntie said the first visit. So much for being smart with the older head...and have their cold rum laced carrot juice. Then there was "Zee," the tall jovial girl that is "credited" with later spanking her wayward lover into a more centrist conformist way of living. Sometimes Shadows looks back and smiles at his Auntie's changing world. She found out that teenagers can be a very different animal from your little agreeable infants of yesteryear. Some of the dramas were not just from the young...even the fathers and mothers were party to these jokes. A certain father was looking over the fence at a dance, pretending he is spitting...then asked the Auntie if she sees her daughter, his wife to be. His fiancée later said he was jealous because he imagined seeing a competitor. An excellent move to remove the competition... That was before Tom the barefooted tom cat, dressed in khaki was trying to ensnare a pretty married Black cat with his, "You want a hard-dough bread and a soft drinks?" Was he kind? Noticed the intriguing "purring" Tom did not say you want a "bun" —colloquially meaning infidelity. That would have sensitized the argument to the un-Christian principles of adultery. Very good tom-*catting*, very good... Some of the older respected church groups were also stumbling in the darkness along the narrow tracks...religion or not, there is that special intrinsic desire with rendezvous, galore!

In those days horse racing at Caymanas Park was just coming into its own. The political debate then was, there should be no taxation on racing because it was just a sport. What utter nonsense! The gambling game became more opened to the public, and numerous "baby feeding" moneys – cash for baby's maintenance— were being siphoned off to the horse racers. There were touts galore giving out secret tips, which never panned out. People were treating jockeys like they were heroes... Racehorse songs were very popular with the Ska beat. In fairness to the songs they were like warnings telling the people that "Longshot bust mi bet," or words to that effect. These were dire warnings not to take the *baby-feeding money* to the race tracks because betting pose a great degree of uncertainty...the refrain of: "...*him gallop, him gallop, not a long shot Lawd!*" tells the final story. It was in this situation that the young Righteous Grass Eater plays a scam after losing the fowl-feeding money and the bicycle on one of these Long Shot horses. He likes talking about horse racing, so his *friendly* tout gave him one of the *sure* long shot tips. We can guess with a high level of surety how that ends. He painfully found out that talking horse racing, and winning at the track were two different things. Because they were practicing Christians, (Most of these people made this claim.) he decided that he should play the part of the returning prodigal. He comes home lying in the field, acting as if he is eating grass. You know, like the mad biblical Nebuchadnezzar in the fields... His sister, Miss Peddy ran for the biggest bible she could find and read some comforting Psalms over his head amidst a lot of weeping for the returning prodigal. Note that the bible size here is comparable with spiritual magnification, because the young and beautiful Miss Peddy had no vision problem. Of course Miss Peddy gave him a sumptuous Sunday's feast before his mother returns from church. There was no more discussion about that "Long Shot" event. The Devil deceived him... Shadows and his cousins always use that as one of those benchmark excuses. Brilliant! The dog eats your home work...too simple, come again!

It was easy to get caught in the race horse euphoria. He remembers how Caymanas Park patrons got caught up in the euphoria by shouting for the leading horse *Rumpeltilskin*, although they have bought the other horse *Long Shot* to win! When Shadows pointed it out to his friend, the friend got a bit bashful and quietly replied, "You right you know. But Rumpel a gallop so hard to the tape mi have fi encourage him on man...!" Imagine the woman still "whipping" her hand in ecstasy, even when the race is over and she had lost her money...

CHAPTER 13

POLITICS and Social classes

In days gone by the local village agricultural workers put the political leadership of Alexander Bustamante and Norman Manley on pedestals. Bustamante was like a savior to the poor people. They talked about Manley in awe; they found his knowledge overwhelming but his life style was way beyond their dreams. They still love him because he was fluent in the English language. They all wanted to be able to be accepted the way he did. They were always talking about some big barristers did this, or did that... Shadows once asked what a barrister was. They could not explain so they again look at you with their usual vacant stare. Anyway, the people really like these guys, but were very aware their present-day politics were a popularity contest between two cousins who they believed were laughing and drinking champagne in private. The villagers often repeated this line whenever some over zealous person got confused and wanted to turn a political discussion into a fight.

"Name-calling" and shielded ribaldry were the manifestations of both political parties during their campaigns. He quickly learnt that Bustarites and Labourites (JLP) were not the same, although they joined the same party. This was a party of massive well-organized grass roots movement with its unionized political wing, the Bustamante Industrial Trade Union (**BITU**). It was here that Shadows first met the indomitable grey haired William Alexander Bustamante. He sat there at a dinner table surrounded by his friends. A vision always played with Shadows mind; Busta was not sitting totally enclosed around the table, but with a space left behind him. Later Shadows believed that was not a coincidence; it was deliberately left for his escape in case of danger. Brilliant! On the other hand he met Comrade Norman Washington Manley, and observed the similar seating arrangements... The People National Party (PNP), "The Comrades" on the other side was backed by the local intelligentsias; make that almost every civil servant. The political meetings in those days were just slanders, scandals, and the inevitable promises of fixing the roads, giving you water and getting jobs for everyone. Once there was a big issue of enabling people to smoke cigarettes instead of smoking tobacco leaves cigars!

"I will give you the capability to smoke cigarettes instead of being poor and only able to smoke rolled up tobacco cigars..."

They won with this rhetoric too, just ask anyone who had smoked the cheap Buccaneer cigarettes during those days, if they are still with us after choosing their poison then.

Whenever the politicians became too obsessed with "name callings" the Briton system would rein them in— little more decorum dear fellows or face a law suit. (There is no safety net or oversight now to rein them in, you say!) The local politicians even started corrupting each other union's acronym. The JLP called the PNP's union— the NWU, a "no work union." The PNP replied calling the BITU, "better I thief you."

That did put an end to that nonsense. Those days you could be convicted for slander. Then there were the banter songs: "Old-clothes-government a whe mi do you? (Repeat)." Or, "When you get the work you sit down on the shovel…" In the olden days the meetings were like a "revivalist" street meeting. The only thing missing was the drums, which they later introduced, but had to quickly relinquish along with singing of religious hymns before the political orations. They were careful not to get too far in the hymn singings and drum beating because the "grass roots" population did not like the trendy mixtures of the temporal with the spiritual. They would sing their political chorus, example *"old clothe government a wey mi do you?"* to various lines. For example one round would be "yaga yaga government…" until the euphoria dies down. Imagine listening to so-called sensible and educated individuals sing to the tune, "hark and spit government…" Shadows is informed that attending political meetings are now like contracting Murder, Inc. because their meetings are like an invitation to mayhem and murder; especially so if you live in the big city. It seems that this attitude had persisted for a long time; giving rise to saying that *the longer one exposed to evil the more callous (or immune) one becomes…* We now see the great outcry for more social discipline. This means reintroducing hanging of the poorer and younger Black males, and the reintroductions of beatings in the schools. There are no mentions of responsible parenting, child welfare, population control or birth control, high school education for everyone, economical growth and justice for the poor.

Shadows recalled earlier days when families have different political views without hard feelings. How about a grandmother handing you your school fee, paused, gazed deeply into your eyes and challengingly uttered: "I know which party you join!" then gives the loving grandparent look of approval then turns away muttering, "Every family have one of those I suppose." He laughed then, realizing she had been listening and watching him…

Politics are now the domain of lawyers, especially those who cannot compete in the legal profession. There are no more grass roots politicians, just copy cats trying their best to emulate the American legalistic political way of life. The downside is they do not have the viable institutions to back them up. This they know and it work for them by not having to fear corruption charges. He contemplated the new changes towards "openness," and concluded that *Globalization* comes with some strange social side-effects. It *weakens governments*; especially the smaller emerging countries. Now everything is run by lawyers hence the numerous *double speaks* and social complexity results in diminishing quantities of grass roots politicos. Shadows remembers the first politician he saw one night at the little village crossroads. The man was clean and well spoken with a very bright gas lamp that seems to quickly banish the darkness. I hope there are no "wise-acre" here asking what is the speed of darkness…! His theme was to ***fix the road and give the villagers water***! And, above all he was easily approachable, unlike the other "big people" who drew an iron-clad circle of aged-respect around them. Shadows was impressed and asked his brother if this man was another crossroad's preaching revivalist. His civic minded brother casually informed him the speaker was a politician and not a preacher. His brother finally crept out of his intellectual cocoon and inquire, "Tell me something; what do you really know?" At that time he could not have a verbal skirmish with his only brother. But what do we know now? Well, we know the populace rewards preachers for speeches (or opinions), and not necessary for their actions, whereas it should be vice versa for politicians. But, oh no, they are preachers themselves. Is it any wonder that preachers are also politicians?

One Rasta was heard lamenting the usage of the Electronic Voters' list as imperiling privacy and freedom. His view is that a government that is always strapped for cash will sell it for usage by overseas government police agencies who don't love us anyway. In this case they could abuse it to assemble a list of people to be denoted as criminals. There can be no privacy there because the Corporation that assembled the list has to obey the laws of their own country in giving the list to their own country if it is required. They will cite the National Security thing, as they always do. Shadows attentively listened to what he knew could be the truth. It is very frightening, but the technology which brings you ease will always bring you some anguish too. What can a human do in the new Millennium to maintain a human presence without this Big Brother effect...oh, and the Big Sister also! The slick college educated lawyers are now everywhere and the poor common sense politicians vanished. The lawyers have many reasons for wanting to be lawyers. Shadows remembered his friend claiming to be frustrated with the social system, so she decided on fulfilling her destiny by studying law. How about the money and prestige? Years later a visitor told this "destiny fulfilled" lawyer how much her body aches from doing her job. The former Miss "destiny" lawyer promptly replied that she would not waste her time listening to the visitor, because her visitor works for herself, and there was no one to sue to recover damages. After a legal career this friend decided she wanted to do something for the little man. (She did not say what size the man had to be.) In her words she wanted to be *faithful to losers in our society*. This was indeed a tactical analysis in human recruitment for a popularity contests. She decided that politics was her bag; therefore she wanted as much admirers as possible. Again, she was successful…had someone once mentioned that democracy is a concept of mediocrity. I suppose we can all say, "The woman was doing her civic duty as dictated by her (*lawyer's*) conscience…" True, but the preachers/politicians already knew voters would rather be momentarily soothed with political speeches espousing idealism and lies than deal with life's reality. Don't feel too bad about political rhetoric because all countries do this. Remember that during the Cold War the US was trumpeting free movement of people between Sovereign States, especially the Jews from the USSR. Then someone from the USSR said alright go to US. Immediately the US started doing a double take about the numbers migrating to the US. Then there were some discussion about migrants coming from Cuba. See what happens in the 80's when there was an influx of Cubans; many may still be in jail in the US, still awaiting their freedom. It seems that their only choice was a transfer between prisons in Cuba to prisons in the US. Listen to political rhetoric, but be cautious because someone's carefree expressions can turn one into casualty. "So don't be an ass; count your costs before mounting your ass." The numerous island born deported criminals being dumped back home to Jamaica, after they gained their criminal habits overseas is a testament to people not understanding reality; listening to numerous lawyers smooth political lyrics on imaginary freedom overseas.

In earlier times, the concept of the Village Lawyer was entrenched in most districts. They were the products of the daily "newspapers" readers. They used information to rule their society. Theirs were never a rule of force. If you were to check these guys they were the ones who did better in elementary schools and on the local exams but never had a chance to excel otherwise because they were poor in cash and therefore lost to opportunities. "Indeed a mind is a terrible thing to waste!" In those days there were no discernible political relationships between those called "dons" and the politicians. Of course the politicians were always promising water and better roads for the community. Are they still doing that now? If they are; then it perhaps better for us to answer no, we don't want that anymore, promise us something else... Imagine using the same old trick on the parents and on the grandchildren generations later! Is this where you don't change a winning combination? The rainy season on the island comes with hardships: inaccessible roads, flooded streams, scarcity of food and fuel, discomfiture by not having dry places and clean clothes because the sun is behind the clouds, and the homes were not centrally heated. Those are the times when we need to complement each other and not to compete. The perennial promises of better roads and water is becoming stupid. Water is a life source; in abundance on the island. One would believe it could be made readily available to the suffering communities after all these years. No wonder there were so many "bogus voting" when people removed the red voting ink from their fingers and vote again; trying to force an election of those who promised them water and better roads. As one dictator, Stalin, is supposed to have said, "It is not who votes that counts but who counts the votes." Is this applicable to the Presidential election in Florida and in numerous Jamaican constituencies?

Now we are told of the Island *white* politician running away to seek advice and consolation from powerful Overseas white politician. The overseas "ginigog" was at the forefront of denigrating and segregating Blacks during the turbulent Civil Rights days. Is this a very contrary move for progress in a Black country? It was not so long ago that people with pale skins held all the top jobs. Are we trying to return there? Then Black competence was never a factor; you have to be white or brown-skinned. This social pattern young people did not understand then, they were not yet in the job market. An example was given when two visitors at his school pointed to the disrespect expected of Blacks towards each other. One was white and very assertive; the other was Black and very laid back. The student then thought the "white one" was the big leader from England as always. It so happens that the "white one" was a minion from some place, whereas the

Black man was the leader many levels above him. A worthy lesson that was clearly pointed out to the students by a socially aware and politically astute headmistress. She was indeed a stalwart! The attitude of inferiority of the Black race is not just a product of the Whites dominance it is well drilled into the children by their parents, especially in the Villages where ignorance is rampant. Children would be castigated if they showed any sense of self respect. Their ignorant parents are always asking them if they think they were "white man's pickney!" It was always hard to maintain a high level of self-esteem within most of these homes. As one grew up one realized these parents had not realized they were still growing slaves for a system that was annulled long ago. One heart still weeps for some friends who had been so brutalized by both parents throughout their young lives. There were no saviors for them then…In later life as one looks at these older folks just ambling about, one wonders if they forget their behaviors. Their usual response is; "But that was long ago!" They are saying it was justified while holding out their meager trembling hands for a donation from their psychologically and physically scarred poor children. The England migration made the situation more bearable for some young people. Some left and never looked back, or ever communicated with their parents. They were just *hewers of wood and drawers of water* for most of them anyway…sad but true. Then there were those men who liked their daughters and hated their sons. Is this a Freudian Oedipus thing? A Jamaican disappointed daughter with deep disappointment, bitterly expressed her view that

Jamaican women hated their daughters; another of Freud's thing again? Some mother's (We cannot find another name here.) are so brutal to daughters we wonder why. They worked and brutalized them like little galley slaves too.

CHAPTER 14

EDUCATION

Getting into the city primary schools in those days could be difficult. Yes, even then an education was a treasured resource because education was not a priority; it was a privilege under the old Colonial system. That system was never meant for the Black colonial people to excel. It was set up to maintain a certain level of competence to assist the colonial masters within the Civil Service. They made it so obvious when they refused to teach the sciences and technical subjects. It was not too long ago that reading was actually forbidden under slavery. Is it illegal now for a parent not to send a child to school? It was not then. Primary school education was free then. People were hungry for knowledge then, and an education was a priority; one of those very well valued commodities. Then there were those jealous people without the chance of an education who would chide, "You believe you a white man." Many of these guys were not stupid; these were bright people who had no opportunity to excel under the old stifling master and servant system.

Shadows first heard the word "catholic" from the villagers. These Catholics were supposed to be "high man" and "deals" –dabbles, with a woman called Mary. On his first encounter with this sinister Catholic power group, Shadows heard his young friends referring to the nun as a Sister Scholastica. He had a terrible feeling of psychic mutilation when he saw this robed being…there were no warm feeling there, just one of dread…a young vibrant soul in turmoil. Perhaps this was an institutional feeling, one that was felt by people like the American Native people when they were forcefully transferred from their homes to remote and inhospitable areas before the British Blanket ruse. There was this chaotic scene of small helpless Black children being rudely bawled at by this domineering white Nun. There were other little ones around with their worried parents too. Many of the mothers sheepishly endured it. Others walked away showing hurt on their face as they maintain their dignity towards the door. The society always whispered about the covert behaviors of the Catholics. The general pervasive feeling then was there is a mystery, which surrounds them, and it was not conceived as being a holy one either. If the domineering nun was experimenting with forced conformity to the Catholic ideology it definitely was not working… Her attitude caused an exhibition of inflexibility among the black skinned people. Of course they already believed that her society was not for them, but for the socially advantaged Chinese commercial groups, which seem to dominate their schools. Shadows now compared his experience to those uncomfortable feelings he experienced while inadvertently exploring dark caves. History claimed the Catholic Church was outlawed in Jamaica 1655-1792…perhaps Shadows should have thank Henry VIII; although the Anglican is similar to the Roman Catholic (RC). He had always ponders their differences except the one called the Pope. During those early days there were no mentions of the latter. There were no Anglican or Catholics in his village, there were only people! Later he was informed the RC believes that the bread & wine are perpetually the body of Jesus Christ, whereas the Anglican believe the wine and bread represents the body of Jesus Christ at a level that depends on a person's Spiritual belief. One of his RC "geneflectors" also stated that it was the RC that introduces Credit Unions to the island during the 1940 to help the poor avoids the numerous loan sharks. That was good; what was the RC's cut out of all these savings?

He then tried enrolling at an inner-city school where everything goes. Here cutting classes and doing whatever you choose was a way of life. Here the teachers were not in command and really did not care; so indiscipline and the bullies reign! This was a sport oriented school where strict academic disciplines were never really emphasized. The headmaster was an amicable person, but his teachers were just going through the motions. He remembers a student bathing in the river and drowning while shouting, "Mi ah dead!" No body paid him attention, they all laughed asking, "Why is he saying *bearded*?" Here, it was not like going to the river in the rural school where there was always discipline. He recollects a student rebellion against a male teacher who was some sort of sport administrator. The rebellion stems from the teacher using rough tactics against a middle grader who rallied popular support against him in the manual training class. The teacher became confused and very concerned about the principal's reaction. He was released shortly after that incident. It was Shadows first sign of people power against the system.

Many students dropped out of school when teachers decided to beat and curse them. A student complained that beating is unnecessary, but he may stand that when his assignment is incomplete, but he refused to be verbally abused, especially when the abuser had no worthwhile information to offer him. "Brutal bitches!" he called them. That was the first time a young man heard the term being applied to teachers. His friend remarked that "De John Crow dem are like ticks on people's backs!" And she had the marks to prove it too. John Crow—local vulture! That word again? That is the most defying word a young child has to fight whoever is perceived as an enemy. A mighty bad word too. Everyone is always whispering that if anyone should hurt you, you should call him a John Crow. Sometimes you better whisper it under your breath or your opponent may *beat you up*, again. He or she may even *beat you up* by looking into your eyes and reading that you are calling him or her that special name. You can just go ahead and *cut your eyes* –make eyes at him or her, but do not look into the enemy's eyes and laugh after he beats you up. That means you are getting some satisfaction from some place else, or you are mentally tripping by calling him a John Crow. In these school systems the bullies are not gender specific. Girls beat up small boys (and even big boys too) as much as they beat up little girls also. And boys generally beat up boys but some boys, the girls know not to *fresh-with*. The general rule is older students do not ever touch a very young child…the whole school will hunt you down when they start to cry! Crying brings the intervention of the authority figures, and takes away the glory of winning. It marks both you and the perpetrator by removing your comfortable anonymity, which allows you to freely commit schoolyard mayhem. If you are the *crier*, you will be constantly ridiculed, and if you are the tormentor you will be possibly ostracized by the gentler part of the school system and watched by the teachers. "Dem know you now man!" He had never heard anyone curse teachers before; not that he knew any *big school* teacher. He knew his elegantly dressed and caring private school teacher, his mother's close friend. But these are big children in a bigger village here using *bad words* too. And they are his protectors! He listens in awe and wonders about his new world, his very new experience away from his mother, quite away from his mother's *frock tail* as they say in his smaller remote village. All these bigger children were praying for *their ages to be up* to avoids the torments, the incessant beatings in school. Is this what it's all about? Fear!

Later he found the city schools were quite different spheres of influences. The bullies were not gender specific here either. The great differences here, was these bullies would draw blood too. Forget about their parents, they were unrestrained and cruel. They did not live in any known neighborhoods or quiet villages either...some were from the mean streets and endowed with great athletic abilities. It now reminded Shadows of the athletic types being shown on TVs.

Shadows recalled the athletic bully girl that is always taking away the younger boys' ball on the playing field. You know you better not ask for your ball until she and her friends are finished. And that is if she feels like returning it. One morning she met her match on the same playing field. It was so contrary, but this time her ball was seized. It was Shadows first sight of a physically stronger male battering a physically weaker female. Unfortunately no one would take up for her, or made an effort to separate them. The children made a circle and cheered them on. The small boys were cheering the male and the girls cheering the female who was badly losing the fight. She was fighting gallantly but was thoroughly beaten as the fight progresses. The children became more subdued as the fight declines into a tortuous one-way battering. In the subsequent bedlam, some gallant older boys mercifully stepped in and separated the fighters. From that day Shadows never really trusted the mass behavior of people in a crowd. That mistrust saved his life years later when people stampeded while at a park...to see a visiting British dignitary.

Later he went to the best primary school and had the best teacher at a school called **Crescent.** This school was a principled institution with a woman as its principal. The focus here was on learning. He met his life long friends here; those whom he competed with in the "private lessons" classes and in other schools. In these private lessons classes a student should develop conviction and commitment to take the Jamaica Local Exams. Nothing was given freely; it was sweat and tears because the 3rd set of that examination could give you a free ride at the teacher's or agricultural college. At this time the village people usually make fun of college and high school people. There were beliefs that these learned people could not do things well. The usual idea was that most of them were just wasting time in school, then come out and laughed in a different tone of voice—a more cultivated one. It was a village joke for people to emulate the learned guffaws of these academicians. Most of the laughter was poking fun at the White colonialists and their Jamaican white plantation owners. Those laughing had never been to high schools or colleges, but they were capable of doing the tangible important things like making a farm produce. Many of these guys were brilliant people in the elementary schools, as these schools were then called. All these promises generally came to naught. Proving the United Negro College Fund's slogan, "A mind is a terrible thing to waste," is the best education slogan yet. They eventually changed the name "elementary" to "primary" schools. But they used the same curriculum… Ever wonder why? Is this where that guy Holmes would say; "Elementary my dear Watson!" Perhaps we should leave out this Sherlock Holmes line and keep to our culture with its deceiving and harping Anancyism by singing, "A will fool you mammy boy, a *harpendal*, a *harpendal* I will make yourself fool too!" We hear the similar stories now. But of course, we are the offspring of our ancestors whom were the product of their times. They were molded in the British colonial crucible of disinformation. Back then it was nearer to post-slavery society, but a more practical agrarian society where the learned colonial bred theorists sat on their island's verandahs or some place in England and talk about the "*bottom-lines.*" Now we see the similar problems with an unimaginative private sector that is unable to create wealth so they employ other unjust and shady means of survival. The country now hoodwinked itself into believing it is not an agrarian society with massive quantity of undereducated Black people. The usual class and endemic tribal separations are still there. We can rant and get into our little polished tea party rave about crime stultifying our economic growth, but it is still unimaginative to expect peace without justice for the poorer Black people.

By this time Shadows have graduated from the nightly mild Anancy stories and frightening ghostly tales to the whispering of rude Big Boy stories in school. Shadows heard one of his "clean" Big Boy stories when the teacher asked how Jesus died. Apparently the teacher hit Big Boy because he did not know. It seems that "Big Boy didn't hear that Jesus was sick, much less to die because where he lives no newspaper passed there!" As if the spate of story types were endless, the Little Boy story was introduced... Shadows later realized that these stories are used to poke fun at the status quo. It was in this context, or frame of mind that he became acquainted with Zipp. She was a tall beautiful Christian girl with what is called a "dry head"—short air. She liked him and prepared special water cups for him during the recess and lunch periods. This was his first "touch" with an open female interest. His social, class-conscious-pretty-girl types groups criticized her interests. They wanted him to stay within their group. He did too, by default. He then had another school road "meeting" while playing ball on the street. His main interests had since left for greener "fields" and there were no other inspiring girl... He noticed her beautiful dreamy eyes, coarse brown dress, barefooted, soft well cared for smooth skin and calm disposition when she *challenged* him for the ball...without breathing or saying a word.

She just froze her action and stared at him. He paused and inwardly questioned, "Now who is she!" There was this deep feeling of kinship; a spontaneous surge, driven by a strong magnetic pull of undeniable attraction as if drawn together and focused in an interplay of invisible energy. Her eyes shone with images of brownish dark crawling tendrils of spidery lights; lights crawling towards him…beckoning him into a land of fantasy…towards some unintended circumstances. He had never planned for this event occurring…He was so easy to placate, more like fooling people who have minimal information and lacks communication skill. He never said a word; he just looks on with the ball high above his head…hooked, but not out…! Now he realized that the altitude, high above his head never meant out of her reach. She had never felt like pressing her advantage and taking the ball at that time and place. She was more interesting in their stirring introduction. This was long after he knew about writing love poems in school… Funny but he had never written any of the sugary "I love you once, I love you twice, I love you next to Jesus Christ!" type poems to anyone.

In those days the institutions worked at a snail's pace; it was almost impossible getting things done through the stuffy bureaucratic system. Getting a passport was a steep challenge. Getting a birth certificate could take an archangel's intervention. Normally, you generally didn't have to go the "archangel route," any of the numerous friendly "touts" at the Records Office would "let you go"—helping you for a fee. Then there was the Income Tax department; it would hold up your tax refunds while their corrupt workers inform you that you have a substantial amount of refund. The corrupt clerk wanted you to pay him to *"let you go,"* according to their corrupt lyrics. Trying to get a student visa? The ease depends on which country. If you are a male and the US is at war then it's easy. You know the drill …expects to give military service. Canada? A well laid back, respectful interview with almost certain acceptance. No threat there. You will have more problems with the Jamaican interview at the Ministry or wherever. You will have to get all these papers for traveling. An intelligent looking police officer asked how come Shadows has all this money; if the government gave it to him. The government in those days, giving money to a socially and politically unknown person; in those days definitely not! They were still polishing up their rhetoric and calling out the Harmon Barracks "bullies" at the slightest ripple to solve all their social ills. The Inspector mumbled how come he and his friends' and family were refused loans! He finally gave Shadows what they called the "criminal identity" certificate while imploring him to give the island a good name, unlike the group of students in Canada who destroyed the St. Georges University computer center. He never mentioned the despicable racial treatment meted out to the students by their professor. He should have asked the Dominican student…

After those island interviews, he learnt that things are done differently overseas. The techniques of learning in a cold New World required new social conformity and a vibrant mindset. It was his first introduction to the big urban world of international gender politics along racial lines. It was a melting pot where island people mistakenly believed that people of their opposite genders and race solely belongs to them. The churning sexual mixture blurs the simplistic islander's idea of the racial and class divide. They now know their former idea that the brown-skinned ruling classes predominates everything was just a myth. Then there was the ostracizing by the islanders of the ruling commercial classes, the Chinese, after and during the devaluation of the island dollars. Here the "inter-color/class/race" rivalry between expatriate groups took its toll on the commercial guys. The docile and apolitical Black masses, specifically avoids commercial dealings with their former island merchants. It appears that the Black grass roots "word a mouth" did them in. It was surprising, because these Black people have never really shown this type of cooperative power before, not in their homeland. On the other hand it could have been envy or retaliation from past experiences.

There were fun galore, but the consequences for mistakes are greater because the institutions overseas worked with greater efficiency. Shadows recalled a very conscientious student warning him, "...the place is abounds with carefree "baby making machines" from the home world where responsibility was most time never a factor." He eventually counseled him, "There are no grandmothers here now! If they are; then they are wearing bright makeup with spike heel boots and staying out late with their new and younger boyfriends. They have no time for snotty nose kids..." Those were about the best social advice he had then. Some of the other "brighter guys" did not listen then.

As one man said, "You take education or take an easier route. Join the freaky long haired Hippy movement (at Bay Street) and just *dropout* as my Guyanese friend did..." It seems the downside came when he finally cried when his friends graduated without him. The Guyanese wished them well, but he felt lonely when he realized how his old parents mortgaged their home to send him, their last child, and their last hope to school. In his parting remarks the brilliant mathematician vowed to go back and finish school. It is not just in cricketer that one has to be careful of the "leg trap!"

CHAPTER 15

WORK

Shadows knew from earlier days he wanted a much more comfortable job than what he sees people doing, breaking stones at their gates to fill potholes on the roads… He tried his hand at learning a trade. That was good but he soon learned that some places treated its workers and apprentices like scum. It was surprising seeing grown men one respected kowtowing to the patriarchal Jewish owner. This was not respect; it was fawning and wallowing on their bellies like worthless dogs. You can love your boss, but looking back over those days it was obvious they were conditioned to respect the skin color. There is a mystique about the name Jew to the average Christian then, and perhaps even now. Jesus the Christ was a Jew, so you expect certain type of reverence from a population unexposed to life's religious reality. As a young man Shadows has to question if this was what it is like working for someone else? When asked how they allowed their boss to talk to them in that way, they used the old familiar and disrespectful Jamaican dodge, "Him don't mean anything, ah so him stay." On looking into their eyes you can see the controlled grief…you have just peaked into their inner mind just before they averted their gaze. One then grows more aware and understands people in the Villages when they voiced their opinion of not working for any white man on their farms. Shadows was told from very young to look

167

into the face of whomever you were addressing. It was an agrarian society that has the dominant landowners with white skin dominating the landscape. The aware people were very conscious of this and prepared their children for the long social battle that lies ahead. Most Villagers could not be employed as domestic servants. Such position carries a tinge of too much subservience for the descendants of formerly rejected slaves, whom were unable to be "seasoned in the Indies;" but unfortunately presently propagates the most odious form of Western tribalism within their ranks! Then the idea of toying with someone else's chamber pot was not too inviting. To be called *"the girl"* was just too insulting to the poor, but proud Black villagers. Many of the Villagers would rather cultivate, and pick fruits on their own land and maintain their self-respect. Now, here is the contrary thing: the term "him a racial boy" meant an individual was a decent person and generally from the upper group. How in the name of whoever was this term ever corrupted to mean this? Any speculation here? It was obvious some one finessed a slur to smooth things over. It worked too! In those days the word racism was not being widely used...and the name Jews was attached to Christian beliefs so the poor people had no sense of differentiating religious meanings. They believed that if you say you are a Christian you are to be left alone because you are on God's path. If you say you are a white, then all is temporally well with you but you will not go to heaven.

Most people then did not know there were poor whites, seriously!

The Rastas were pragmatists. Their doctrine did not believe in the European "pigmentation superiority," or the infallibility of those materialistic "church goers" who claimed to be Christians. The "Dreads" were quite aware that the "other colors" were of the same opinion, in believing that the *sanctity of life* only applies to them, and to them only. Hence the conflict between the societies at large because the Rastafarians were believers in truth, and they also always cherish their children…in that case their views would be passed on. They knew they were Black, and were never part of the ruling social class. They were not afraid of knowing their history or being called Black. Neither were they afraid to be stamped with an African identification. Because of these "defining" qualities they were socially ostracized. Imagine "learning trade" in this type of social cauldron. Shadows decided to change gears and go somewhere with a little more enlightening view. People then believed that any person showing compassion for the Rastafarian ways were exhibiting extremism and antisocial behaviors. The society in general believed the Rastafarian views on Christianity were warped and scripturally impure. Then there were those Jahs who preached that the Ethiopian Haile Selassie was a god. That did it for the society…Later, Shadows recognized why so many Blacks refused to be waitresses; they were just too tired of being the usual "serving classes" for the other races…

Next stop was the Post Office, at Orange Street with its little petty bureaucrats. Here the young guys practically tremble whenever a certain "senior" guy comes around. He may suggest that you go on the "red wheel"—being the postman delivering letters. This was a class conscious job where those called *clerks* were the masters and the *non-clerks* were the peons. This division was so strictly enforced that later it reminded Shadows of what he read about the Apartheid system in South Africa or Separate but Equal in the USA. A Black ex-soldier that was in England was one of the groups called "sorters." His rigidity in upholding this status quo was frightening. He strutted around the place, his arms at rigid attention by his side, telling his workers they should not be joking with the *clerks*. "You should know your stations in life, ole boy!" He was so pathetic at times. On the other side another ex-soldier of the whiter-shade (and of course he got the better sit-down job) was always muttering that he was an Italian from Milan. He called himself the Milan boy. It was really fun time here. Then it was time to leave to another group; the Civil Service where name dropping is the order of things. Everyone here knows, or pretended knowing a "*tapanaaris*"—a well connected and elegant person. It was a fun place that creaked with complacency and mediocrity. This is a place where you get little pay but much respect and great visibility. Here inhabits people that you read about. School ties are eternal. Manners and appearances are very serious things. It is a social twirling world of presentation and façade. This is a place that they insinuates *fashion* and *freedom* are closely related. It was during this period when the white and brown-skinned Jamaicans were slowly leaving the Civil Service to their Black compatriots. They found out that working in the emerging technical fields had more opportunities than the somewhat sterile

Civil Service with its fading British decorum and tightly managed pay structure. Money by this time was visibly eroding the rigid "honor roll." Anyway most of them had their positions through the "ole boy system" whether they passed their exams or not. They were *skin-type* selected more in accordance with the famous line from the movie, Last Boundary: "If you are white you are all right, if you are brown you can hang around, but if you are Black you have to stay in the back." Then there were gradual changes during the advent of the electronic era. All copying machines and other computer peripherals were called "IBM." No, not Intercontinental Ballistic Missiles…those were probably in the drawing board stages. Many of these brown guys were never found in the teaching profession either. Perhaps they have no interests in teaching Blacks…just too clannish, or there were no desire to be typecast as serving the Blacks! So many unanswered questions…

A new stint at JPSCO (power generating company) brought a different outlook on life. This was a place where money and promotions are of real importance. People were not about social showiness; they were about material substance; the big money, the big new shiny sport cars, and the beautiful homes in the upscale neighborhood. It was here Shadows learnt about fierce competitions and hatred among workers. Even friends will take advantage of you when the enemies are numerous, and being popular is more important. Here he met the humorous pair of "Cracky"— slightly mad, and "Mellow"— meaning he is soft in the head. One of these puzzling fellows got involved with a cunning "operator," the security guard at the gate. The guard decided on running his own brothel at the guard house one night. Apparently, the "puzzling" fellow was short of cash; so he *"lamped"—tricked,* her by giving her only one shilling and nine-pence because that was all he had. She gave him a *brawta* seeing that he works there, and she already had many customers from the police and soldiers detachment that were then used to guard the power station. Unfortunately for him, she gave him *something* else too. He had to visit the doctor, and was almost disciplined if others had not openly testified of not seeing him at the guard's house. That is what he got for urging others to partake in their paid sexual orgy. The final saga was a trial to determine if the guard, a professional little liar should retain his job. It appears this perpetrator had done this before at different companies. It was quite an eye-opener to the social behaviors of the outside world. Shadows had a first hand view of what a court case could have been. He had read so many stories of high profile cases where long convoluted arguments were used to arrive at a verdict. An old friend once told him that many of the decisions were unjust; they were political and could generally be deduced by a probability curve. He had no opinion what a probability curve was then. His older friend slowly explained to him that the powerful groups generally get all the best court decisions. It seems the judicial group was part of this ruling class. Now he is reading that one of the Zimbabwean government officials is implying the same thing in their fight for land distribution (more like *reclamation*!) to the landless Black African poor. They are always having "some a dem long arguments" with the same predictable results, *the poor Blacks lose again*!

SPIRITUALITY/MYSTICISM/OCCULT

People are always dreaming. One "rum-head"— mildly boozy, stalwart claimed people are too idle that is why they have so many dreams. His version is that they spent too many hours sleeping instead of seeking wisdom. His friend, the one who called her alcoholic drinks a *mother's breast* theorized the inhabitants have too many heavy meals late at nights…and most of their dreams (or astute visions) are always about some spirits telling them future things. This gave them a feeling of invincibility as they waited for their dreams to unfold…here come the nightmares when this predictability fails to unfold. This infallibility belief is very common among the young, and sometimes results in sadness as experienced by Shadows' friends Wicked Roy and "Crab Soup." Wicked Roy tried faking out his friend by passing off his girlfriend to Crab Soup. Unfortunately for the socially well connected Wicked, the low keyed Soup eventually raised his level of acceptance, and put forth such a good performance that the woman starts becoming attracted to him. Yes in a big way! The versatile and well liked *Wicked* started to have doubts about his infallibility when the lady invited the rejuvenated *Soup* for numerous discussions. On one of those hot nights, the Wicked's grandmother asked him to buy some ice. On his way back he saw the well attired, and now newly respected *Soup* in the darkness quietly knocking on the lady's door for admittance. The jovial, but somewhat now jealous Wicked hid among the rose bushes in the garden, changed the ice from his left hand to the right. He then surreptitiously used his cold left hand in the darkness to touch the superstitious Soup's cheek. The amorous Soup vanishes like lightening on the far horizon... long before the mildly jealous but more mischievous Wicked realized his friend ran away and left his bicycle. *He was too concerned that the man took the surest mode of transportation available, his feet.* The playful perpetrator looked all around in the darkness but his friend had vanished, totally vanished from the scene. The Wicked became alarmed and confused, so he went back and secured his friend's bicycle before someone *borrowed* it. Many days passed and the Soup was not seen. The curious and concerned Wicked decided to look for his friend. He found him in bed among many rows of multi-colored candles surrounded by his family. A red-robed Revivalist was trying to remove the *sickness that overtook him when a spirit from the grave (But where else!) with its cold and clammy hands tried bringing him down in that wicked woman's flower garden.* The astonished Wicked just listened and watched the Soup's family burning incense and "rubbing-him-up" – massaging— with Cananga water; chanting purification rites, wearing their clothing backwards, then setting an altar with bloodied white rice from their sacrificial rooster, while reading verse from the Psalms...only the destructive sounding ones he observed! The Wicked got confused; he tried telling his friend it was him and not a ghost, but his sickly friend kept saying he knew the Wicked was *just trying to cheer him up.* The Soup's family thanked the now contrite Wicked for his attempt at cheering up their sick relative... They eventually warned him to *keep away from the woman with the rose garden...now they know why he is not bothering with her*.

"Island people" are dreamers wherever they go. An expatriate school dropout basketball player turns ghetto-playground hustler returns *home* seeking treatment for some *bad vibes man*, according to him after the following dream. It seems none of the main stream "schooled" –bible schooled—religious fire and thunder North American Black or White Christian preachers could fathom this mysterious dream. No, they did not asked for the biblical Daniel, or Joseph...! Mom and dad with island roots are always sending their dysfunctional "overseas" children "back home" for some primitive "home remedy." The Black playground cheater dreamt he was playing a demonic White basketball player. He had to play by the rules or suffer death. He wonders if he wins fairly what will happen to him with this confounded and belligerent spirit holding all the cards to his continued existence. As he thinks about his predicament, the taunting female Spirit momentarily stopped, stares at him before pivoting to take a shot. It understood what he was thinking and just warned him to be very competitive in the game or stop playing in this dimension forever. He instantly understood its meaning that if he were trying to let the Spirit win by not giving his very best effort, it would be interpreted as cheating. It eyes were luminous yellow, its jaws were tensed as if chiseled and its whole demeanor was defiant when it turned to take the shot. It missed! It rushed for the ball…but it went out of bounds. He was momentarily stunned that it missed…he got a new lease on life, but for how long? Time is of no factor here. He has the ball now; you missed Miss Spirit he told himself with glee…she will not be telling him he cheated babies out of their food by robbing their fathers at basketball… She sighed and glared at him with flaring nostrils. This was no joke, and this is not a simple dream either. Now she smiles and they now both understood her mission for his life's dispossession. Or, he now understood that this is a different life where to lose here is the end of game for him. There is no waking up or going to the next game. He missed his son already… "Gambler!" said the voice. "What?" he lost concentration and repeated as she deftly plucked the ball from his hands and accurately shoots it through the hoop. How many times in his lifetime has he distracted his opponents causing them to miss their shots. He always wanted to play in a final game, he dreamt many times of playing in the big times; claiming he never got an opportunity… "Until now," the voice chimed with a mocking dissonance to the words. Then there were shrill laughter as she turned her back and walked away to start the next series of play…

When Shadows told a friend about what he now termed his friend's "weird ass dream," his friend decided it is a demonic *drop pan* dream…they each bought number 13! Big surprise they won a shilling's worth. Now, how can one explain this mystery? Oh, yes, certainly message from the Cosmo. You have to remember that numerous drop pan buyers (losers) were always complaining that "…if they buy *Jerusalem*, the

contrary Chinese man would play my *happy home...*"
Could this be like the Chinese man who decided to
cheat the old lady at *drop pan*? It seems this old lady
always catch a "chuppence"—three pence worth of the
play every day. The conniving Chinese banker told her
he is leaving the next day to live in the parish of St.
Thomas. To ensure no one wins, he decided to play an
illegal number, 37. He knew no one would be coming
to St. Thomas to track him down. Now, there are only
36 numbers in the drop-pan play book. (The number
36 means old lady. As if you didn't know already).
The next day she caught him preparing to leave town.
She bade him a fond farewell, and asked what he
played. He smiled and surprisingly said, "I played 37."
She laughed and said, "Mr. Chin?" They both laughed
because they were really old combative friends. He
wanted to beat her just once. They both knew that was
an illegal number. She finally said, "Check you
book...mi ketch *quattie worth*—one and a half pence
worth!" She did too. Now what do you think; she was
the reincarnation of the white demonic basketball
player, this time transmigrating to a darker shade of
pale? Seems we are all colorful dreamers. As the
affable mortician in town once said:

"When mi dead Congo worm will come tell me..."

CHAPTER 16

HOMAGE

In paying homage to those departed that made his world he bowed in remembrance of their deeds, whether it seems kind at that time or not. He recollects his old sick uncle borrowing money, and Shadows wondered if he would be able to repays it. The old sick uncle was right on time with his payment; a symbol to pay your own way irrespective of circumstances. He remembered friendship, love, understanding and help from all the males. It was instilled in him that families should stand together and we certainly did. There were hard times but they just could not last because we share the hardships together, thereby minimizing its impact...there were more abundance of better times too. In looking back over the years and remembering the Special One who said, **"I will always be around you, and will speak with you but you will never see me..."** It seems as if someone will always be there to take care of the innocent; as shown in the Joslyn's effect. Shadows cast another glance at his history, trying to decipher when a young aware person's life changes to a more serious level. Is it when one sees a mother giving birth...through misunderstanding when told to call the doctor...Is it the diverse ways that a child grows up? There are so many unsolved mysteries in life, especially to a young mind. To focus on any specific one is to lose the joy of traveling through time.

There are so many defining moments in a life time…
Which one is more important, pick one.

One defining moment is when a mother tries
bathing a child for the very last time when she saw his
springing pubic hair on a chilly morning after the early
morning "diesel" passed, going to the town. He got
cold water from the portable pump across the train
line. This was his morning preparation for school,
which was about 2 miles away. As he hastily prepared
his bath, praying that his loving mother this time
would not try to help bathe him. He was reaching that
stage of puberty when he believes he has much to hide.
The much includes a trace of public hairiness that can
only be seen if you are wet. OK, alright now, everyone
has a limitation in time… As on a cue he heard his
attentive mother coming around the house to his little
private area! At least he wished it were. Some
practices seem to die-hard. One of those is an attentive
parent's desire to always help their child. At this time
many guys in school were practicing; "filling the wash
pans, pretended to bathe and then emptying it." The
water was just too cold in the early mornings. It seems
the word got around too… She grabbed the towel from
the cold water, soaped it and began vigorously rubbing
his upper body. When she reached his legs she
momentarily paused, but continued observing while
scrubbing in a subdued manner. He watched her
although his vision was far away across the hills. She
abruptly threw down the wet towel in the soapy water,
and left with a pensive face. …her silver bangles
jangling as she tried drying her wet hands by wiping
them together… He observed her motion through a
vision rather than his physically focusing on the

incident. No words were ever spoken except her terse, but curt, "Bathe your own self!" She moved away from the privacy of that corner of the house. Away from a life that typifies a young son and a loving mother…leaving him to a final physical independence. Whenever he reviewed that incident he always wonders if he won his freedom or lost his innocence that cold and foggy morn. Changes are necessary, but some left indelible marks on our existence. He remembers her not giving him eye contact…just straightened her back, squared her shoulders, sighed and quietly strides away in the misty morn, back to the old kitchen as if exulting with triumph saying: *I won. I brought him up to an excellent stage of early manhood.* The unfortunate thing for him she died a few years later, just before they started to develop a more adult mother and son conversational relationship… Shadows reflects on the saying that "good people never live long;" if that is so then longevity could be a spiritual system to give humans a better chance to redeem themselves.

In the departure from the childhood dependency stage, the "grown ups" generally manufacture different communicating ways of talking with you, for example: "Last night mi dream say…" They are always dreaming something they wished to tell you. Shadows remember this was a communicative way for a certain Spiritual Mother. This pale-skinned clairvoyant Reader woman would quietly sat in her cozy rocking chair…partially closing her eyes, but being aware and obviously listening, acting as if using the *third-eye* with its ensuing panoramic views… acting as if peering into inner space; enwrapped in clean warm clothing with her numerous helpers at her beckon and call...her huge beautifully old chipped blue mug resting invitingly near her elbow with steaming, strong, hot black coffee. It just sat there adorning the rough wooden side table. She sighed and gave one of her trademark mystifying sighs in her "unknowing tongue" that usually solicits a reply from one of her servants, or other minions who listens attentively to such sounds. She rocked back and forth then sipped her coffee...praising its taste, not the cook. She does not praise people's efforts because it has a way of showing favoritism. There are too many people pulling on her for her to choose an individual. There are the usual "spiritual yard" rumors that she already gave up warm desires for her husband. Her second "revival" was about loving the family, specifically her children and grandchildren. The husband is the financial stabilizer, but he is presently no money earner. Those days have long past when he traveled away with a brother-in-law to various countries to work. Intellectually he is sound and aware of the children's slovenly attitude. The old man considered them indolent, too dependent and wasteful. As he grew older he carefully watched his families grow with numerous grandchildren living under the same roof. He then made financial plans never to again be in poverty. He recognized his children will never be able to help him in his old age. He gesticulated under the tamarind tree, and pledged that he will never let anyone point at him again and say' "You see that man there; he was once a wealthy man!" He was correct!

Shadows remembers the class consciousness of the society where a young woman refused friendship with the old man's son. Apparently this classy woman saw him speaking with his wife to be, a lower class woman according to her. She refused his advances and brazenly told him they were not of the same category if he is in friendship with that type of woman. Shadows later realized that a happy and fun life can easily kill you as much as an unhappy and hard one can. Very hard and very easy are excesses at different poles of the life's spectrum, and all excesses are bad. How about excess cash? Isn't that dangerous too! Shadows recollected that these were questions that were always asked by so many money hungry people. Many persons have what can be considered as the *excess cash*, but they are still in the intense-care wing of some hospital wishing they were poor and healthy. Money has too much power, and too much power is bad. Life gives and it takes too…now what are we willing to give up; our cash or our lives?

CHAPTER 17

BUSINESS

It took Shadows several years recognizing that business people controls the country. They have more money and therefore more power. It was no wonder the Chinese could afford to comfortably live apart from the rest of the society. Money has too much power...for pure visibility and ease of operation it has just too much power. It is the reason why the USA is the dominant power in the World. Long ago they understood effective business is power. As one beaten down American ghetto dweller once said, "The name of the game is power, and that is *mo-ney*, and if you have no *mo-ney*, then you haven't a-ney (any power)."

Shadows looks at the young woman in the street of this old small town, flaunting her sexuality as she searched for power by selling clothes. She stood askance looking into this sturdy man's moon-like penetrating brown eyes with her huge, round, and attractive docile brown eyes. She takes on a flexing stance, with her clothing goods draped across her left hand, periodically searching his face as if looking for an emotional niche to latch onto. With his confidence at a peak, he emotionally plays the beneficial dictator, possibly to openly show his power over her. She probably plays along in this emotional tryst to soothe their passion as others closely watched their interplay in the old, noisy, congested and musty market streets.

In earlier years, on another street, in another musty, but larger town Shadows is reminded of irate sellers chasing a terrified country boy. The peddlers cornered him in the old cemetery; the same one that Buff is so fond of talking about. The poor slender, young fellow was so distraught that his face showed absolute terror. He was sweaty, panting with his pants almost dropping off his slender waist. As a child Shadows watched the advancing noisy *higgler* women unsheathed their numerous sharp knives and slowly encircled their quarry. The poor tired boy in his despair leaned against an old inscribed marble tomb stone exposing the words, "Rest Beloved...," panting as he watches them through frightened wide brown eyes. The din instantly recedes to only the sounds of harsh breathing, the breath of a tired boy being cornered by a group of bloodthirsty females. They were almost touching him with their knives. A frightened Shadows ponders whether they were going to carve the frightened boy's body as they do their pumpkins when preparing it for *leggings*—mixed vegetables for soup. The boy just watched them with his sagging multi-colored shirt soaked with sweat. The crowd paused and made an intense eye contact with their quarry. "Wait!" someone shouted. "We have to be careful we can't just kill him like that," echoed the burly higgler nearest to him as she brandished her sharpened big blade knife a few feet away from the boy's neck. "Him a country boy, ah whe him know 'bout thieving in a town market?" shouted a shirtless handcart man from the back of the mob. "Dem ketch the right thief; this a no the right one," shouted a younger higgler briskly running down the street. Instantly a countrywoman came down the street bawling, "Clinton! Clinton! Clinton!" All eyes turned in her direction. She was sprinting with her long dress flaying all over the place. There were no controlled or civilize motion in her strides. There were heightened levels of urgency. The woman practically leaped over the crowd and hugged her son with such fury; pushing him tightly against the marbled head stone, now like a premonition exposing the final inscription of "RIP;" as if it was their last Earthly time together in the old cemetery. Then with an anguished face, as the snoot ran down her nostrils, mixed with her freely flowing tears... the mother looks at the women with their weapons so close to her son and kept hollering, "Murder! Murder...!" That shriek of doom blanketed the old cemetery; reverberating throughout the tall cool tamarind and the prickly acacia trees like a final weapon of mass destruction. The mob jumped back giving mother and son some breathing room; now too frightened and chastened to speak. The child and mother just crumbled there, silently hugging and weeping with relief. All the higglers began crying... A policeman arrived on the scene (late as usual) and warned the crowd about its action. Shadows still sees this incident as the *cornering of the young defenseless innocent.* The higglers tried blaming the young man for running, but the police brought up a good point when he replies that if the boy did not run they perhaps would have killed him in the market. It was his first time in the town. His mother brought him to town to show him the city, which nearly cost him his life.

Now, there are sellers, and then there are those *original* sellers! Shadows remembers his uncle, **The Pharaoh,** coming to the aid of a distraught man in the streets. The dark skinned woman held this young slender brown skinned man in his *trousers front*. Her grip was taut and as one could say decisive. Taking care of the family jewels was not part of her concerns. It was dark. She was barefooted, short, serious and sturdy. He wore broken down brown shoes with well-worn heels. His pants were slightly below his hips. And no, he was not one of the local "bop boys" wearing his pants low down on his hips! The shirt looked soil and a bit oversized. He was scared. He remained quiet, staring straight ahead into an unknown point in space. He had no fight left in him. It was obvious his fighting spirit left him on the edge of tears. The only communication between these two was immobility and silence. Her face shows rage. His face shows the shame and despair of the illicit open street conflict. They stood near the store almost in the lights from the bar... The Pharaoh left his store and enquired what the matter was? The woman brazenly replies;

"He owes mi my oil money yah a sah!"

The man said nothing but swivel his head with emotionally vacant eyes, like a dumb robot to acknowledge her answer. His uncle asked if she could forgive him his debt. She retorted no, because he lied to her when they negotiated. His uncle paid the amount. She immediately released her client, straightens his clothes, gently kisses his cheek and quietly told him, "I don't hate you. We can do business again because you are a good boy." The *buyer* breathed a sigh; the *vendor* then vanished down the dim street, in the direction of the old cemetery while telling my uncle thanks. The *buyer* did not thank my uncle, but my uncle cautioned him to be more careful of his actions while he is in town. Shadows knew most of the higglers in town so he said to his uncle, "But this woman doesn't sell coconut oil?" His uncle quickly reprimanded by saying

"Don't be foolish; use your senses!"

Yes, he had really learnt many important things from his uncle, the versatile Pharaoh. He reflected on his drinking the strongly high proof "**kullu kullu**" estate rum before going to bed. Someone mentioned that a "tot" of rum before bedtime gives a good rest. He had never had problem with sleep, but inquisitiveness calls for an experiment, yes a rum induced experimental rest. You know, never had one of those before…ahem. Shadows then started taking small doses of rum from one of the bottles. One night the Pharaoh came home and exclaimed, "What is happening to the rum in that bottle?" He pours out some in a bottle stopper and lit it with a match. A bluish flame enveloped the bottle stopper. The "Egyptian named-One" then pointed out that if the white rum can catch fire like that; just imagines what it could do to your young stomach. His voice was quiet but firm. The young nephew understood the demonstrative message, although he glibly said to himself that he was not swallowing a match with his booze. Anyway, that demonstration put an end to his nighttime sampling. Even decades later he maintained this distaste for quaffing rum…

Then there were those long "Partners" (*Pardner*!) Not the present day computerized Pyramid schemes that seems to proliferate the North Coast. In those days no one was too keen about hypothetical mathematical series and random queue payments. They all wanted well-defined series of payments…that gives a greater level of predictability and greater mental comfort. You should not make anyone have to come and ask you for their "pardner draw." There were many unflattering stories about dishonest *pardner* people, generally the "bankers" that did not give others their *pardner* draw. It seems that people are always "throwing their *pardner* hands" but never ever gets a draw. Shadows eventually realized that whenever they get the draw they remain quiet. In that case you will not ask for a loan. It was always, "It's for my partner money." "How come you never get a draw?" "Mi wi get mi draw in time." The next time you ask, "What happens to Daphne?" "She got her *partner draw* and gone (*does the serious Daphne walking*) to England."

Presently Shadows is hearing that the society is in turmoil. There is a view that women are having the greater access to better learning and therefore better jobs. There are numerous social theories that women are using their sexual prowess on the numerous weak minded and irresponsible decision making men who are always ravenously in the market for younger and younger teenage schoolgirls. The women also played their parts by using snide and derogatory remarks about the men who tried to avoid their advances. Many of these relationships have short lives. How often have we seen a man and his relatives berating their helpless mates? Ever heard the rude and cold suggestion to:

"…dash dem out, dash out her things in the yard!"

It seems the women are now doing this as they flexed their economic muscles. One woman claimed she was not a cow, and therefore has no "pastoral experience!" She was telling her lover and his relatives that she was alone, and he cannot now just excuse his discomfort by ungraciously remove her to a large open place like a pastor. Shadows sportingly envisioned a pastoral scene, but he knew the affairs unfolding before him were "no picture postcard village" affairs. This was reality where a woman was being discarded from a place that once gave her sustenance. In his boyhood and adolescent days there were no well defined paths of feminism and women rights. It was said that some of the wives of the Colonial governors like Lady Huggins had made conscious efforts to help the downtrodden women. Numerous couples were living together without "jumping the broom." It seems like *jumping the broom* is a wedding rite from Africa; practiced by Blacks American slaves. (Now the Whites could not afford to let them have a Christian wedding vow. Then the Christian system would have to consider the Blacks as humans by equating love and dignity to them in the repeating, *"What God put together let no man rent asunder."* If that was done, how would they easily sell them separately? Would that be flying in the face of the Almighty?) Anyway, in this type of patriarchal society a woman could toil for years with a man without financial benefits. Her years of service generally *went for naught*. If there were not much accumulation of wealth, it seems the society always culturally bequeath the bed and the furniture to the woman, but not the cows, the house and the land. Oh yes; the women get to keep the children too! Many Black women were generally looking for brown skinned men with straight nose and the "good" (straight) hair...their desired pigmentation characteristics, their imaginary tools for merging into the "other" social levels. Numerous men were of the same opinion too. You see their moms inculcated them early that Blackness is bad; so many of them plotted against their heritage, and ended up as the little "maids" or the "yard boys" with numerous poor brown-skinned disadvantaged children after being kicked out from the "big yard." Now they are shoved towards the Black group to be consoled and raised by their shortsighted and racist Black grandparents.

Shadows is reminded the social place girls were forced to occupy in the society. They were a disadvantaged underclass, a position forced on them sometimes by their parents. Many of the girls were turned into *"little mothers"* for their siblings; being robbed of their childhood as parents tried eking out a livelihood. They were always being trained for the domestic market: sewing and cooking. Birth control was partially non-existent. He recalled how young girls rebelled and left their mother to reside in the towns after complaining of the restraints at home. On the other hand, some made the migration the other way to the country parts. The teen age years are so full of changes. He remembers his cousins, as teenagers *looking wood*—gathering firewood and having her younger country sister carrying the firewood and the machete. It seems she could not afford the cool boys seeing her carrying wood on her head. These were some of the annoying situations for a young woman with a high spirit. Even going out were challenging for the girls. The mothers would set them hard tasks to accomplish, and then reneged on their pledges when the tasks were accomplished. Shadows watched many young lives destroyed as women tears fell like water falling from a leaf after a rain storm as they drained their sorrows and wished upon a better future while toiling through heartless relationships forced on them from an early age. Some feminists are saying that if women were running the world there would be no war. Perhaps the name "No War" would be the name of the war, like the name "WWII" is just a name. But in truth, we do wonder if they could have done worst than the men...

Those were the days before Shadows heard the Chinese saying empowering women that:

"Women hold up half the sky," is attributed to a Mao Zedong quote, but the news is that the Chinese villagers still favors a male child. It seems whenever it comes to people's freedom like empowering women words are cheap.

The social classes have drastically changed since he was a child in elementary school when "*leading cow head,*"—leading a yoked cow pulling a cart was the most demeaning of all the rural low class jobs. They would decry low ambition boys by saying, "You see how you worthless, a cow head you a go lead!" Then there would be a trailing off of the voice as they turned away muttering about some Mr. such and such son. They do not want you to repeat anything negative they say so they mutter it to themselves. He observed his first "cow-head lead;" a young shy older boy who knew he was being scrutinized. He sat there resting on the roadside, and believe it or not, he was smoking a cigarette. But that was for the up scale Backras, or the aloof car driving Black professionals. Shadows was young, but the social image of a cow head lead smoking a cigarette was confusing. He wonders what type of upside-down confusing society is this. Sitting before him is the dichotomy of social contrariness. The cow-head lead was smiling as the young schoolboy Shadows watched him. The mental image still sharply plays as if it were today. As the old saying goes, perhaps the young cow head lead was at peace with his dharma at this time. Undoubtedly the young cow-lead was providing him with images of a society gone mad with its divisiveness. He would not dare tell his mother that he saw a cow-head lead. It was not an appropriate learning tool for a young child to repeat, so filed it away as a future negative reference to avoid. "Push hand cart" *was* the downside of living in the urban areas. "*De bwoy* a push hand cart a town!" was a vicious social scandal. This is probably as bad as leading cow head in the rural areas. These occupations ranked right up there with being a thief. The socially conscious villagers failed to see these as occupations. Most of them made no provisions for their children, but they were quick to adjudge when their children tried eking out a living the best way they could. Attaching such stigmas was enjoyed by the many simple minded people as they followed their class-conscious colonial masters. This point was clearly made when a rowdy family tried to get their pit latrine repaired…the men who usually do the job refused. They passed the information to their buddies that these people mocked them with the usually contemptible phrase; "I know you…if you even half masked I know you!" The family suffered discomfort and humiliation because no help was available to them. "We do not do too well in our own waste!"

Then there were the street hustlers, "samfi-man" — confidence man in the 3-card game with his usual contrived antics of allowing you to win a first contrived game; then bang you are hooked. Or the other "hooks," of turning sideways to spit while his friend shows you the winning card. People then also developed the new scam, of touching your moving car and then lying in the street claiming your car hit them. They were seeking 3rd party insurance money. The motorist's usual outcry was, "Reverse and kill him; it costs less." One man got up shouting "Unoo murderous frigah uno…you would a kill me fi save the white man some money. Ga long!" Then what about a Obeahman burying a skull in your yard one night; then inveigling you to let him show you that someone is out to get you? Now it is said they are using plastic skulls for this little caper. Welcome to the plastic world of the 21st century. Shadows theorized that plastic is cleaner than the older sacrilegious way. Then the newer trick, which is played especially at the tourist resorts, is a person saying he knows you from the country parts, while telling you his vehicle is out of gas. He will show you a vehicle but he doesn't own it!

CHAPTER 18

JUSTICE!

Judicially, things have changed and the Gleaner newspaper is not taking its moronic pleasures in writing about young Black men; preferably being tortured with cat-o-nine tails in prison or being charged for vagrancy by walking into some white upper class neighborhood. Shadows recollected seeing one of these tortured victims with scars all over his body. His family sent him away for recuperation; thereby ridding the family of a visible social stigma. Then there were the dark corrective notions that telling a male child about "Formatery" School would break his spirit. No one ever tried explaining what it is about. They did not know; their only answer was, "Is where bad boys go and it was in Stony Hill." Apparently there were no checks and balances after some outrageous apartheid-type judge passed his usual sentence of incarceration and other physical tortures. Could it be that some of these unconscionable judicial decisions have come back after all these years to haunt us. What type of persons did these brutalized people produced? Just remember this; your progenitors were all mostly quiet then, so are you now in the face of increased corruption, mounting injustice and increase brutality! It seems prolonged force and injustice begets magnified counter force…

Police then had no guns; they walked beats too. He witnessed a couple riots that were started by political zealots (a fashionable term for idiots) when the visitors from the City try showing off.

Now things have changed so much that everything is now foreign-based. Even agricultural people are presently fretting about the Y2K problems, and they have no machinery! The Healer placed the machete across her shoulder, as they walked through the cow pasture. He instantly remembers his old friend, Herman's tale about the Mysore cow's attack. She brought him back to reality by jokingly ponders if the machete was going to function. Shadows chuckled wondering why these foreign people write all this mysterious and funny stories. She asked, "What is a computer bug anyway?" She waited for a reply, and then added, "I have never seen any on the island!" Shadows replied "We have something in common there…neither have I!" They both seek redemption from ignorance by agreeing that bliss through ignorance is not necessarily contentment because the mind yearns for knowledge and understanding. She knows about indigenous herbs and plants. She told Shadows a certain tree was called, "Old woman's gummaw," an herbal plant that have edible fruit or leaves when cooked. "Old woman gummaw," he repeated to himself wondering what the word "gummaw" means. His mind played the associative mind game in wondering if gummaw was associated with "mummaw," which locally means mother. He usually called his grandmother "Mummaw." He smiles in remembrance of his softly spoken grandmother as his mind ran through various combinations to affix a root word to the word "ummaw." He resigned himself to failure as he put it down to just another word meaning that is lost during those horrible cultural mutilation of the Middle Passage forced migrations. He listened to her discussion on newly found medicinal herbs and plants. It seems that new and wonderful plants have existed around us without our knowing its benefits. We were so caught up in laboratory medicines that we drifted away from traditional ones. On the other side, it appears the knowledge base for traditional medicines have been eroded with the help of the Europeans' great push to *white-washed* all vestiges of the African knowledge base. Anyone working in the herbs and cure business would be suspected as being a Obeahman, or a Spiritualist. A Spiritualist was legal, but the legal definition can become quite a concern. The police would definitely plant a spy to trap the practicing herbalist. This has its good and bad sides too. The main propagated idea is, if it's environmental, then it is African from the Slavery days, and anything African is no good. He was delighted hearing the new found source of medicinal herbs. He now wonders what the big pharmaceutical firms will do. Will they try duplicating these plants genus in the lab, or grow them in abundance with their "wonderful" quick growing fertilizers that will eventually poison or depletes the herbal potency and then depletes the soil nutrients after a few years. Well, in that case instead of boiling herbs, back to the confounded tight capped pharmaceutical bottles. It seems all these manufacturers consider older people expendable. If the older folks were not considered expendable, why are pharmaceutical manufacturers making "fool-proof" safety caps on their bottles, which older folks cannot easily open? The effort to open a bottle will give older or sick person an anxiety attack, even a fatal heart attack. This must be a design to rid the state of older people who no longer paid taxes, or cannot "walk fast"—move around briskly.

As he listened to her tale of social progress with roads, transportation and more efficient water sources; she paused, and then looked at him. She broke the silence by telling him that some resources are still scarce. He knew that, and told her that contrary to what some people may remember, commodities on this island were always scarce. Shadows recalled his early childhood trek for water at a place the locals called GOD Hole! As a child then, he knew nothing about the other water accesses except from the river. The river was dry. He followed the group by passing the abode of the mysterious *"wrapped head"* man they called Ebenezer, the *God Hole Master*. As a child he knew there was something strange about this man. People always speak about him in hushed and respectful tones. He was always jovial and polite with his booming voice.

He first remembers traveling with a young upbeat group to this underground water source, deep within a dark cave. There were mysterious gurgling sounds coming from deep within the meandering, damped cavern as the intrepid and thirsty group cautiously made their way towards the receding water. The older ones were firmly grasping the younger ones hands. The fear etched the faces of the groups…he cannot now recall the names of the few female stalwarts who talked and laughed courageously, but with trembling voices as they warily trudged towards the receding water with their flickering smoky kerosene-oiled and coconut-bough torches held aloft. They timidly passed the *safety points* of the two rocks dubbed Joe Louis & Max Schemeling who he found out later were pre-World War 2 heavyweight boxers. Shadows recalled approaching the water where the shrieking and gurgling sounds intensify. Some of the older ones then asked that all the children are to be held at the back to enable them an easier access to flee in case of danger. As they timidly walked around a corner in the dim cave Shadows, remembers asking himself what is making that heaving sound. His childish mind then could not picture anything more dangerous than darkness. Oh! But this was long before listening to ghost and Anancy fables. And also long before the Europeans' dragon tales of St. George, or even the *smoking* one called "Puff the magic dragon." So a moving realm of thick darkness it was. Finally they reached the water. It was a bluish shallow stream in motion, heaving to and fro, while slightly splashing on the moist rocks on either side. They quickly filled buckets and departed amidst much bravado…of some one shouting "De river a come down!" – The river will be in spate.

Shadows next cave encounter was with bats. That was the time he mistakenly walked into a cave by parting some vegetation at the cave's entrance. The light startled the bats in flying into a random pattern…or so it seemed then! Shadows immediately dropped backwards through the vegetation at the cave's mouth to safety. It was not a good experience at all to be awakened from your childish exploratory reverie by numerous startled and smelly black (or other color) bats fluttering across your face… It was a very quick glance, but it seems this was not a color integrated cave! This again brought up the desire for information, but not knowing what you are going to use it for. Bats and owls were always coming from that cave location during the nights. The owls were called Screech owls. Whenever they made a sound during the nights the villagers would respond with, "Salt and pepper fi yuh mumma!" –salt and pepper for your mother. It seems the owl's sound was a death warning; a very ominous signal if it ever passes over the house. No one ever mentioned why "salt and pepper." No, Shadows had not heard about the Rose Hall's Annie Palmer, "old hige" witch tale as yet. And he was not part of that mature collective to make an enquiry. You can just imagine the fierce reply, "A weh you a try fi do; get in a dem fore-eye man sitten?"—what are you trying to do; get into wizardry.

The third cave experience was while coming from school. This was a new school where the rules were quite different. The headmaster (for need of a better description) was a little *"beating"* maniac. One has to give credit to the headmaster. He had good discipline and good academic standards according to Shadows' dad. Here the pranksters were older boys from an adjoining district. They lured the younger schoolboys into a cave already occupied by other hidden pranksters dressed into ghoulish outfits. While in the cave the guiding pranksters extinguished the light just about the time that you could see the "ghouls" coming from behind the rocks, or jumping from the roof. The children tried to escape in the darkness and some bashed their bodies on the rocks. It was scary then. On looking back on the scene now, Shadows had to smile, and agree it was dangerous, but it was well done by the older boys. Anyway, the joke got out of hand and the perpetrators got scared, and quickly tried calming the situation. Their effort to calm the situation magnifies the youngster's fear. When the pranksters tried holding and comforting the smaller children they practically freaked out believing that the unearthly demons were touching them. Shadows can still remembers the cries for help. He felt insecure in that cave in knowing he was not with his old dependable childhood group. His brother was there, someplace outside, but that may be too far away. (Did his brother actually hear about the plan?) Anyway, in the cave he then felt he was among very dangerous strangers. In his childhood heart he instantly revisited the clinical coldness of the nun and put her in this dangerous human category of the taunting cave inhabitants. Her face emerged through the darkness with her staring unwavering blue eyes as if challenging a youthful heart to try and leave without submission to her will of spiritual destruction and serfdom…

Then there was the *"quick sand"* episode when his mother was washing by the river. He knew about the warning signals on land, but had failed to heed the similar signals when it occurred in water. There were an abundance of fishes and shrimps in the water where a large tree had been removed. The space was quiet and crystal clear with little meandering paths on the sands…like small tracts where the big crayfishes and shrimps traveled. It was too easy, trying to snatch the resting crayfish at the bottom of the still pool. Shadows remembered thinking how can so many fishes be here.

It was like having an abundance of fruits on a tree during a scarcity. What would cause that; something is a deterrent why the fruits were not reaped. A young friend standing a respectable distance behind him calmly mentioned, "…them say dem have quick sand there." There was no urgency to his voice, just a bland statement without any vocal emotion. But then, what is *quick sand* anyway? He was too engrossed in catching the big crayfish to make an inquiry. As he reached out his hand a warning voice from somewhere inwardly cautioned him to be careful, but he had already made his forward motion towards the big dark crayfish and a watery grave. He stumbles and the water reached his throat and rising towards his mouth. He gulped and tries holding his head high above the water line! Now the crayfish was no longer important; the water was rising above his mouth and he could not swim. Where was his little friend? His mother was up the stream washing clothe. His mind recognized that his mother too would be another problem: she told him to be careful. A quick wisp of darkness enfolds him and he stepped back from the shadows of oblivion…he was in the shallows again. He crouched, put his hands on his knees, bent over and coughed while looking at the soft loamy riverbed where he once stood on the edge of nothingness. There his footprint failed to make a ripple in the treacherous sand. The fishes and shrimps had just merely crawled away to a safer location as if to lay a more effective trap for another unaware victim. Shadows recalls that was the first time he had the freedom to wonder away from his mother. That freedom to choose almost put him in a shadowy world. Independence and freedom come with their own responsibilities. He did not tell his mother about the incident, but he vowed he would tell all his friends to be aware of the quick sand where the dead tree stump was removed, and he did too.

CHAPTER 19

JOB INTERVIEWS & HOME

It is really true that separation has its surprises as shown when the time comes when Shadows looked across the seas. He had a surprising statement during his farewell meeting when a friend chided him for leaving the island. During his settling period away, he recalled replaying his friend's statement while searching for a place to live. When he asked a recently arrived migrant to recommend a place; the migrant pointed to a Caucasian woman saying, "You see the White Gal with the *caut-ta*—a soft bundle— pon her head over there; she has a place." Shadows found out she was a daughter of the rich and well connected. Her blazing brownish luxuriant hair was bundled high on her head, showing a brownish freckled face with round deep blue eyes in a gaunt face. Her skin tone was milky white. He had never been around this pale-skinned type before, but he certainly reminisced on the encounters with his jovial schoolmate, Gloria from the parish of St. Elizabeth. This one indeed was not her. Gloria was short and robust with numerous freckles. This one was slender and frail looking with dark cosmetic traces around her staring eyes. Her teeth was very attractive, evenly spaced and somewhat whitish; a great departure from Gloria's. Gloria was kind and very personal… She likes him but his interests were then elsewhere. When she vanished from school, she then vanished from his life. Now he wondered what

203

has become of her. During that time his main interests had also departed to another school. In those days there were great drives to marry professional women, nurses especially. The nursing profession then had a mystique all its own. The teaching profession did not carry the influence a nurse did. Trainee nurses were generally taken from the high schools, and therefore many brown skinned women were nurses. Got the message there...economics, color and race! Years later numerous Practical nursing schools sprang up, and began training everyone who was willing to pay the fee. At that time a massive influx of Black skinned women applied. There were outcries (from the nurses too) that the nursing profession is being ruined by admitting these callous and under educated women. Remember what the UK trained nurses told the recruiting government minister, Wills O'Isaacs? Shadows remembers a former schoolmate, a nurse who refused to converse with him. She excused herself by saying she could not remember him. These types of childish behaviors were prevalent among the status seeking classes. Shadows called that encounter the "erratic farce" of not remembering former school mates. Professionalism was tied to skin color, generally. Men wanted brown skinned women...a psychological and economic profile developed from slavery. Some people would give their souls for brown skinned type mates whom many times treated them like sub-humans. At that time economical prowess and social acceptance weighted heavily on the skin colors, and everybody wanted better things so we can understand the dilemma for poor Black people with that certain ambition. "I do like you but you certainly cannot help me!" The powerful commercial groups like the Chinese and the Syrians were not in this social mix; they were powers unto themselves, and rigidly stayed within their racial bounds.

Now he is in a different country, and facing his first interview before a strange woman… She sat there in silence, dressed in black, staring at him with a dark grayish parrot perched on her left shoulder. The parrot's claws were clawing into the slight bulge in her beautiful black dress. Her face was well lit, with riveting hazel eyes, with straight nose over a small relaxed mouth. Her hair was long—hippie type length with streaky grey. The background lighting was of a cool white translucent shade. It seems someone had paid good price for the lighting arrangement. Shadows equates the scene as one straight out of some Buccaneer's era. It seems as if she took a respite from breathing. Her attractive chest heaves…ever so slightly. The computer on her desk just went into screensavers mode displaying, "Time to choose Life or Death, NOW!" It reminds him of tales of Captain Teach, or the one legged Long John Silver with the talking parrot on his shoulder. No she had no black beard, or flaming matches dangling from her beard. She has no discernible beard. It was obvious she was tall. She fixed him with her unblinking eyes.

Over her head was a sign saying, FEAR = False Evidence Appearing Real

To break the silence Shadows said, "I am here…" The bird instantly craned its neck in a riveted one-eyed sideways glance as if to better focus its eyes. Shadows remember stopping and wonders if this was another of his experiences with mystifying animals that inhabit landlords' homes. Now, this gives him a greater impetus to own his own home, and don't bother with renting. He immediately recalled the occurrence with that beautiful white tomcat with its mysterious piercing blue eyes, dominant personality, and very long tail delicately playing with a whirring fan while watching him through the vanes. The only thing left for the cat to do was ask if Shadows wanted to play. That was some troubling episode... He is definitely not in a mood for that unnerving scenario again. The bird jerked him back to reality by saying, "You will like the place; it is nice..." Shadows remember saying, "What!" to no one in particular. He was not expecting to be addressed by some preening greenish, curved beaked bird. He likes animals, he wished they would just stay within their humanly accepted-dimensions when he is around. The woman just continues staring straight ahead, through him as if he was transparent. There were no smiles on her face. The image of the spinning ceiling fan was reflected from her left eye glass. This spinning image attracted his attention, and he imagined a blurred path of stirring coolness surrounds her. He theorized that beyond that limit, nearer to her is where danger lurks. He wanted a place to live, but he is cautious; he knows we at times violate our spiritual wishes with our manufactured stress resulting in a mission statement of self- destruction. He is still coming down from the stress of that obviously trans-dimensional cat! He drifted away from the metaphysics and reclaimed his cultural roots, his comfort zone, with, "Hmm...trouble de a bush, Anancy bring it come a yard!" His braggadocio of calling on the foreign patio to confuse the mute, throwback Rose Hall-type ("white witch") and her loquacious bird did not seem to faze either of them.

The darn bird repeated its information, "Woowee! The place is nice I said." Shadows gathered his composure and became more business-like. He was careful not to act belligerent by inquiring if it's a bird's brain or a human brain doing the rental transaction. "Who is doing the business here?" Shadows asked. "'Who,' is not here now. Talk to me!" He realized the bird raised its voice. Was it alarmed, angry, or just plain rude. Where had it got so many words? And in constructed sentences too…! He remembers becoming silent, watching the parrot moving sideways on the shoulder of the stony faced woman with the silent demeanor of a well-dressed up mannequin. He guessed they are a ventriloquist act but he wonders why the *witchy* outfit…Witch Bender! He then advised himself to be cautious because some casual experiences could turn one into a casualty.

She held up her hand and started talking on the phone. He paid no attention to the conversation. As she continues the wording and sentences started filtering into his awareness. The dialogue was strange (and unclear):

"You can have both our double-bottoms. Why do you want her semi-bottoms when you can have our double-bottoms? We certainly have it here! To get into that you would certainly need an end dump… How about doing this on my low beds? Lovely, flat beds then…my preference too. With all this type of action we will set up invoices with all the gals concerns. We can do that in a van too. We will put the gals to work on the flat beds and then do the transfers. We will keep

207

track of our actions by using day tags… 18-wheelers, 10-wheelers…We will supply everything. No we do not supply Lot Lizards! Laugh…."

Shadows sat there listening to the conversations, drifting between thoughts, wondering what type of business is she in. He just could not put a spin on the conversation. Here he was being baffled as his mind took time out to readjust its bearings. It comes like he was listening to someone singing the ditty: "Hill and gully rider, hill and gully…" Is she a "front?" A front for what he asked himself! He smiled; thinking about an earlier blunder into a Cocoa Cola "distribution" shop, asking for coke after a very long trip. The server then asked which he preferred. Now, there was only one type of Coke. His friend smile and said, "What, any type bottle or can." The server stared intently in his eyes and a few more people materialized and started looking very inquisitive. A man went outside, looked around, came back inside, shook his head, laughed, whispered to his friend and then gleefully offers a free box of Coke… The man was quite firmly against accepting payment. It was obvious he wanted us to leave, and quickly too! Welcome to New York, now go home Island guys and *decipher* the signs correctly…

He finally met her other parrot at home screaming, "*Eeeat herr!*" She claimed it is saying, "Peeterrr!" its name. Really? A bird calling its own name, or is it issuing a command.

HISTORY

The media was rife with Western white propaganda, especially as it was soon after the end of the WW 2 and the beginning of the Cold War. The news then was from the *rinsed-white* daily newspaper and sometimes from the few radios. In those days, radio owner would have to pay licensing fee. There were numerous unimaginative antenna camouflages among the trees by using thin wire as antennas for better radio receptions. It seems no one wanted to pay license for their radios. The problem here is you wanted to boast about your new radio, but you could not crank up the volume because someone could hear it and may report you. Then you would be taxed. Everyone was spying to see if you have a radio. They just want to hear the news. The first known transmission was called the ZQI in about 1940. This was the forerunner to the radio station RJR, and then Redifusion in about the 1950's. They had some very boring songs in those days. Things picked up later when a cool white D.J. at RJR called Charlie Babcock, with his audio moniker, "This is CB the cool fool with the live jive!" CB took over and started spinning the latest Rock and Rolls, which actually started a "radio listening revolution" on the island. This is the same guy who is supposed to have called one Mr. Chen Yapp at about 11:00 PM offering a promotional gift. The sleepy and annoyed, but well focused Mr. Yapp asked him where he was.

CB tried soothing him by quickly telling him that he was on the air. The irate Mr. Yapp replied that CB was lucky he is in the air, because if he was on the ground he would have kicked him in his ass! Some fun those guys were…

Prior to CB's cool time, heavyweight boxing was the big radio news. The world heavy weight champion Joe Louis was then still a revered icon by all groups. Again it seems we could only have Black role models in the physical arena showing brute force when entertainment is necessary. It was tantamount to Blacks now playing sports on the TV. Shadows recollect his changed social awareness when a boxing ring announcer introduced one boxer as, "…Ezzard Charles, the Cincinnati Negro…" Shadows then understood that there were serious color divisions between groups in the US. In his country no one ever refers to another person as being a Black person from the village of Riversdale or otherwise. They would use his or her name. He and his friends generally categorize people in social classes by wealth, and not necessarily by color, or racial groups. That one announcement opened a new phase of understanding about the US and the dilemma in South Africa. The latter was always never openly mentioned; thanks to the gutless daily newspaper. Then later comes the British radio propaganda: "This is the BBC calling. Here is the news read by some (male Briton…)" It was never generally a woman!

There were not many positive Black models to follow, and those who made it practiced the schismatic "old school boy" cronyism. Those preaching equality and Black dignity were ridiculed by other Blacks. It is indeed uplifting to see the Rastafarian movement is now upgraded from being a derisive outcast to become the dignified savior of the Western Black heritage. This movement has motivated the population from their racial lethargy to keen racial activism. There are still some concerns, but there are numerous compliments and it is coming from the right source too. At this time when the Western Black population is calling for reparation from the West. Shadows wonder why they are not calling for reparation from the Arabs and other African states too. The Arabs are notorious slave traders. Is it not so? Then where does the other African slave dealers come in? Are they now all broke! They are still collecting money, especially from Western Blacks for showing their notorious Elmina Castle, at Cape Coasts, Ghana where they tortured and raped our fore parents before shipping them to the West. Shadows recalled his youthful discussion with an astute Rastafarian *bretheren*, Ras Rabbi the One-I, who claimed his lineage was from the kingdom of Kush. He met this strange man while on vacation in another remote village. The man was quiet and much respected by his neighbors. It seems the villagers were quite afraid of him in the similar way they would try avoiding the local "Revivalists." Because the latter communicates with unseen powers whether good or bad. They all referred to this man as *"the war-man;"* no name as usual, just a label. His fruit trees were loaded; no thief would be bold enough to venture into his yard. Or even to legally pick fruits hanging over the fence on the roads. As a visitor Shadows picked an orange hanging over the road... The older ladies on the road were alarmed and started praying, begging him to spare Shadows for he was just a mere innocent "*young pickney boy who no know whe him a do.*" Shadows laughed. Ras Rabbi the One-I tilted his head backwards, took a slow deep breath and frowns in his grey locks. The frightened older women gathered around and pushed the younger girls behind them, the older men stay back from the circle, but tightly gripping their sharpened machetes. It was indeed a power struggle between the newly acquired city attitude of the young and the entrenched old occult beliefs of this hilly agrarian district. Shadows laughed and said, "It is legal because it is hanging over the road. Do you want me to pay for it?" Shadows continues peeling the orange, and then begins eating it. One of the nearest older ladies was alarmed, and tried *boxing* it out of his hands screaming, "You wi dead!" Her brave effort was in vain; too slow and erratic, probably because she was trembling "*like a bay leaf.*" It was obvious she would never have done too well in the old schoolyard "*box out nuh touch*" game. Her face was like a death mask when she again stamped her feet and shrieked, "Mi say you wi dead!" Her last scream was high pitched; one mirroring total fear and futility with an opened mouth emphasis on the final word, *dead.* The shrill sound wailed out along the hills as if calling everyone to prayer. Shadows eats on. The mysterious man softened his glare as if receiving an inner message, straightened his posture, sighs and slowly turns away. The crowd watched the smiling Shadows; probably expecting his death throes. A gentle barefooted slender woman wearing a long calico dress muttered, "Pickney what *gwine* happen to you now?" There were tears in her eyes. The young

Shadows was very conscious of the lady's level of empathy when she reached for his hands, then whispers to her daughter to bring her the blue *ointment from over the back door*. She rubbed Shadows hands and "crossed ten"—made the X-sign on his forehead while she repeats the 84th Psalms. Shadows smiles and played along while eating the orange. The crowd questions him why he came there *just to eat an orange*. Finally they came to the conclusion that *"they put him so."* He remembers looking over the fence and sees the smiling face of the mysterious One-I standing there shaking his head. There were no mystery there, he was laughing at the crowd. The next morning while passing, the One-I asked Shadows if he wanted some orange. Shadows said good morning and thanked him. The mysterious and well traveled One-I started a conversation by telling him the villagers were well meaning people, but they are very ignorant and way too superstitious. It seems he reside in England for a long time and had seen military action in Africa, Europe, the Mediterranean and the Middle East with the British West India Regiment (BWIR) in WW1. He recounted the harsh and discriminatory treatments overseas by the British officers of the *colored* only BWIR. His main topic was what he called the Halifax Affairs where many soldiers died through coldness. It seems he believed the British contrived to kill them with coldness by not issuing them warm uniforms as were done for the white troops. The crowning insult was the lack of welcome when they returned home, because the white colonialist groups were afraid of their newfound Black political awareness. He said all the ex-soldiers were continually *shadowed*

213

everywhere, meaning they were being watched for any sign of rebellion.

He reiterated that he was always a free man. To prove his point he interspersed his discussion with references to other historical Black groups throughout Black Diaspora. He gave Shadows a history on Kush. He told him tales of Pun, Ghana, and the Ashanti (Asante) heritage… He then enlightened Shadows that Ethiopia, which he claimed were never overrun by the Moslem because they gave rescue to Muhammad and his followers in the early days of Islam. He then commented that Ethiopians are never generally seen in Jamaica, although many of his brethrens are still wishing that they are of Ethiopian descent. He referred to Marcus Garvey as the *"most excellent enlightener,"* who learned from an Egyptian. To the young Shadows that sounds a little contrary. In those times everything about Egypt, or the Pharaohs, or the Pyramids were mysteries. Remember the Egyptian priests could turn staffs into snakes when they opposed Moses. The Pharaohs were considered wicked because they had slaves and worshipped idols. No one linked this wickedness to the enslavement of Blacks by the Western Christian iconoclastic worshipping whites!

Shadows was then intrigued, not by the reference to the great and most excellent Mr. Garvey, but to the reference to what his youthful mind conceives to be the Biblically mystifying Egyptians. At that time Shadows recalled being a bit suspicious because he had never read any such thing in what he then viewed as his revered historical bible, the "West Indian History and the "Builders of the Empire." He voiced that opinion. The One-I one sneered and replies, "The rulers dem

write your own history to suit them! Selah." It was
then that Shadows really started thinking about society
and its two-faced, black and white, true or false
historical omissions whenever it is political expedient.
"The One-I" then rambled on about the complexity of
the Christian religion as viewed by East and West.
According to him the orthodoxy of Ethiopian
Christianity is different from Western Christianity. It
seems the West sees Christ as both a man and a GOD.
In the East, the Ethiopian Christian sees Christ as GOD
only. He equates thinking with power. He pronounced
that Western chattel slavery magnifies with American
colonization and the Portuguese trade expansion when
the latter gave guns to certain tribes and tilted the
balance of power...but he also intoned slavery was
always common in Africa. Shadows had heard years
later that slavery was in Madagascar until the 1980?
The "bretheren" decided to talk of an historical
anthology of positive-minded "brothers" like
Boukman (Bookman) Dutty a Jamaican that was
credited with starting Haiti's revolution. He told
Shadows that Haiti's progress was impeded after
Emancipation because they had to repay the French
150 million francs for their investment purported to be
lost during the upheaval. If they failed this repayment
France would have hindered them from getting
international recognition. Historically it is said that
France then recognized Haiti in 1838 in exchange for
150 million francs to gain international recognition.
USA gave accreditation by sending Frederick Douglas
in 1862. In Haiti's political upheaval it seems Henry
Christophe and his then buddy Dessalines sold out
Toussaint to France where he died in prison. (History

215

recorded that Toussaint wanted to regress to the old system of slavery when France decided to again return to slavery.) In other words the Western oligarchy made an example of Black Haiti to dissuade other groups from achieving freedom from slavery through revolution. It seems that the US was afraid of having a slave rebellion on their hand. (Although so long ago, it seems this policy of hindrance is doing well today. It was done in the Security Council in the late 20th Century to the Black South Africans.) He vilified the US by pointing out that the first man killed in their march for freedom was **Crispus Attucks** another Black. He then went through an anthology of Black freedom fighters. Some other local guy named "**Plato**," supposed to be a Spiritualist that lived at Moreland Mountains, Westmoreland and was executed in 1780. The One-I laughed for the very first time when he said, "Plato liked rum, and so was captured when he was drunk. Cursed everyone in sight' saying he would send hurricane to destroy them. There actually was 1780 hurricane devastated the island..." Then there was **Tacky's Rebellion 1760**. A Caromantee slave on the Frontier Plantation in St. Mary. He too was killed by Scott's Hall Maroon sharpshooter. **Sam Sharpe's Rebellion**, 1831. Hung in 1832. Trelawny Maroons taken to Nova Scotia 1854-65 then to Sierra Leone. He also touched on the Chinese immigration from Panama... It appears that some of the Maroons from Halifax were then sent to Sierra Leone because they became too aware after the war. It seems the British freed slaves from the US during the 1812 Revolutionary War for their willingness to fight, or for their labor. He then cited a strange name, the

Garifunas (Black Caribs), on the Caribbean Coast in Guatemala were deported from St. Vincent. It seem the slaves found a useful co-existence with the aggressive and freedom loving Caribs.

He reiterated that the Whites seem to be willing to abolish slavery, but he termed the Motherland Blacks seem too willing to continue it. While watching Shadows' eyes he enumerated that Denmark abolished slavery in 1792, the first nation to do so. Mexico had emancipation in 1829 the first nation to do so. Cuba import slave up till 1865… Brazil halted slave trade in 1850 but then abolished the trade in 1885. He then brought up a new name, "*Quilombos*" saying they are runaway slave communities in the Brazilian forests. He said whites will generally used Blacks to fight their battles when the going is rough, then later discarded them when they believed the Blacks are becoming too aware. He did not have many kind words for the **Buffalo Soldiers** of the segregated US Army regiments established in 1860. "Were they hunting buffaloes as food for the white troops?" Shadows remembered asking in a puny and nervous voice. "You would believe he laughed, "No it was more profound…they were taming the West for the westerly migration." He then explained that it is recorded the Indian nations of the Cheyenne and the Comanche called them Buffalo Soldiers as a credit to their bravery. In 1866 there were 4 cavalries and 2 infantry regiments used by the Americans to fight another minority, the Native Americans… He claimed these killers upgraded the American West, but helped in committing genocide on another struggling and destitute race that was also fighting for its freedom. He finally glared at the young Shadows asking if Shadows believed such action help the Black race.

Shadows realized years later he was trying to find out innately whom Shadows really was then…

Their time together helped Shadows in his understanding why he sees the Indians at the movie as the real heroes…they were fighting for their very existence. He referred to the Roma (He said people generally called them Gypsies.) in Central Europe who came from India between the 9th and 14th Century. They too have been considered "outsiders" for over 500 years. This is very similar to the appraisal of Blacks in the Western World. The Indian caste system then came under his scrutiny. He said it is imposed by birth, uphold by the religion and expected of their tradition.

Why are we always mimicking the brown-skinned upper class? The Rastafarians enlightened us that the society was giving us *false imagery* and thereby propagating our *self hate* with negative thoughts. In introspection, how many times you have heard, "Mi nuh trust anything black!" coming from a Black person. Did their parents inculcate them to remember the deceptive African chiefs who sold them into slavery? If so then what about "Mi nuh trust anything White?" Get the point! There were no mentions about slavery, or racial disparity from the rulers. These issues were considered offensive and insensitive; they tried to finesse these issues as a non-issue whenever it suits their purposes. Acting as if they were repelled by it whenever they appeal to our better judgment not to remember the past. Shadows body became chilled and constricted because he was a product of the island divisive geopolitical and racially ethnocentricity in believing that we were then better than any other Black group. We then usually decry them by taunting: "If they were that aware then they would not be making all those mammy-type deprecating movies with men straightening their hair, trying to be white." Imagine, now we straightened our hair and try making or getting into making derogatory racial videos. And now, generations later, we claimed that we are better educated and more aware too. We are just more isolated, indiscipline and more prone to violence and hence *hurrying* our own destruction. We are definitely not better!

The One-I shook his graying dreadlocks, scowled at Shadows and uttered how American Blacks are the world's most racially aware group. Shadows realized the old political warrior's scowling mood swings were a tool to enforce the idea that this was no "banjo-playing and mento-dancing" joke. There were no smiles between them! When Shadows looked at the old man's face he saw the importance of their meeting etched in numerous wavy lines across his forehead and shadowed by his graying locks. He was sweating but his eyes were fierce and forceful. Shadows was riveted to his seat on the rough bamboo bench. There were a momentary silence; he could hear his heart racing as if just finishing the century-yard dash. There was a pause... The voice in his head calmly said, "Do you understand?" He blinked his eyes but the old man was not speaking. Neither was the voice Shadows.' Could the voice be that of truth and justice? From what the One-I had said it seems all the other races except the Whites are losers, just like in the movies... if this is so;

he wonders who wrote this universal script. At that time the young Shadows has never met an American: Red, Brown, Yellow, Black or White. The old man continues; chiding that Caribbean people are not generally concerned or outraged about slavery, racism or inhumane treatment to themselves or others. Is it because at this time, they are the ones meting out their inhumane treatments to their under educated darker skinned person? In the early days whenever older persons is asked about slavery, they would give a blank stare. They actually had no idea what you were talking about. Because they have no idea they tend to become *complacent or* angry. Their anger was not at being the descendant of slaves; it was an anger of being unable to answer a child. Shadows believed this was one of the reasons why the British gave them limited access to information. It kept them unaware, docile and happy in their ignorance. Even until this day when there are international conferences the CARICOM groups, comprised mostly of the descendants of slaves and indentured servants, do not seriously raise questions about racism at the Durham conference, in South Africa, on the reparation for slavery. They are still mute on inhumane treatment towards their own people. Is it possible that the long "clinical exposure" to everyone's brutality have eroded their spark of humanity? Shadows is not saying that they should linger in the slavery mode, but they should go forward and recognize that history has a tendency to repeats itself. (Ok, here now, will the dinosaurs return!) The Black World it seems has left all the racial struggles to be fought by the conscious African-heritage North Americans. It seems that Blacks respect have been seriously compromised by their leadership struggling to maintain good relationships with the IMF, the World Bank and other lending institutions. Does the struggle with Mugabe in Zimbabwe giving lands to the landless Blacks come to mind…?

Shadows knew that today's often-bantered ideas of ethnicity were never discussed, and even then it was a problem. There was no racial awareness, except among the Rastas. It was then a class structure that was generally based on race; more like a glossed over Brazilian-type social structures where racial discrimination is purported not to exist. With the quantity of working poor, it seems like the slaves were not released, but increased…over the years. Slavery is never over because the *carchie* –steam whistle on a cane factory blows the *crop over*—end of yearly cane crop. There are all this justification for slavery, but the end result is racial hatred of the Black race. The US justifies slavery on economic grounds, and not on racial arguments. Perhaps we should converse with the Grand Dragon for clarity, or ask Marcus Garvey what he said! Shadows always wonders how the Africans justify it. It is rumored that some of the South African diamond mines are owned by Zionists. They too were a disadvantaged group for millenniums. Are we now going to ask them, "…how about reparation?" Quite likely the **Huguenots'** descendants also own these mines too. Are these the French Protestants of the Reformed Church by **John Calvin,** 1555, who were hounded out of France by the Catholics? Are they an offshoot of the Protestant founded by Martin Luther 1517 in Germany? They have all experienced the human repressive cycle, but they in turn are doing it to another weak and unpopular minority group. They too were hounded out of France (Europe) by the dominant power of the day, Catholicism. Then again some said Protestantism was never a spiritual exercise, it was started as a political construct to counter the power of the Catholic ritualistic hegemony. There are now Black shouts of, *"We get no recognition of our genocide…"* But how can we; when even in this day and age our cowardly and heartless Black political representatives shy away from sending high level representatives to the UN conference in South Africa…

After all these years Shadows can look back with respect on their last discussion about what the knowledgeable Ras Rabbi the One-I's on **Henry, Repairer of the Breach trial** and the continual government interference after his 10-year sentence. The Gleaner (article) once stood up and questioned why they can't leave the old man alone. Shadows was truly impressed but the One-I was truly dumbfounded! He had expected no justice or comfort from the classical planter-type, one-party media and their carbon copy judiciary system. There were numerous prohibitive laws for the poor Black masses, but not the brown and white persons. It appears they generally have no obligation under the laws, so there was no penalty justifying their changing their attitudes towards the poor disenfranchised Blacks. If they were in court it is quite possibly they were the ones prosecuting some poor person. As one old lady once repeated, "they were the judge, the jury and the lynch mob" They were indeed the overpowering *ginigogs*! In those days people would put up their *guineas* for their "doctor bill," but never a lawyer fee. Yes, **lawyers** were then called solicitors that charged guineas instead of pounds. We could say the lawyers found an easy way to charge their clients 5% more by not using the usual pound sterling. Shadows recalled the "Big people" talking about court cases where they addressed the judge as "Mir Ranna." He always wonders why these people known as "judges" were always called Mir Ranna. It was years later he found out that the Villagers meant "your honor." On looking back he truly understood why the well informed Ras Rabbi the One-I, found the newspaper's stance so unbelievable. Perhaps we should check their records to see if anyone stepped out of line, and was censored (or executed) for that article!

He remembered the newspapers were always taking up for those in power, always. Perhaps this attitude leads to the attempt in overthrowing the Colonial government. During that time the propaganda of "poisoning the reservoir" was everywhere. Everyone walking at night claimed to have seen the insurrectionists, except Shadows. The rewards for bringing these guys in were laughed at. The idea that these guys were dangerous was like a joke. People party more and laughed at the system even more. The trouble was no one ever takes anything serious, not even when a destructive hurricane threatens. To prove this point: once there were numerous hurricane warnings. This man securely battened down his family inside. The hurricane came while he was outside securing the last window. His children saw him running from the flying zinc outside. They just laughed at their father. It was a joke to them to see their astute father running aimlessly to save his life. Their mother was too petrified to do anything, except put her hands on her head and shout, "Him a go dead out de!" To try and opening the door is not part of her thinking process. Then again perhaps she has a different agenda? Shadows always wondered why hurricane warnings were never taken seriously. There is always the usual infantile statement, "Man a try to fly in a God's face. Him no know when God a come!" A hurricane warning always put people in some type of party mode then, so they do not batten down their windows and doors. Neither do they make any other preparations. Whenever their home is destroyed they are running to others seeking refuge with the general excuse, "I never really believe them." On the other hand if it is thunder and lightening, they are shouting with their eyes and hands raised to the heavens, reverently shouting, "A hear you Lord! A hear you!" It seems that different energy warrants different transformations. In looking back on the enjoyment then, it seems there was an overriding desire to embrace the naturalness of freedom, or perhaps a just youthful zest for chaos…

Now here he is again with another Dread from almost the same era, but in a different village. This time it is with a "throwback" Rastaman that is wishing for the often bantered "good old days." A surprise; how far back he wants to go…touching slavery! Whereas the erstwhile social activist **Ras Rabbi the One-I** sees things in a balanced spectrum; this aged Jah is lamenting how the Blackman always have the right views, and *they* did us wrong views. Are we still asleep? Whenever Shadows brought up some of the negativism of the Black group the *brethren* waffles.

"How can we correct our errors if we fail to acknowledge them?" For instance when Shadows asked about women in Africa, specifically the **Trokosi,** "wife of the gods" practices where little virgin girls, after seeing their first menstruation are given to cultural priests in Ghana to be used as their wives. These children are given by their parents to atone for "wrongs" done by their family. Such family will have to continue doing this atonement thing generation after generation. "Is this a form of generation of feminine slavery...?" Again the Dread waffles and made excuses, "It is their culture." But so was slavery in Africa! Shadows knows that we should not stay on the fringe of our outer awareness, lamenting the past because we have no future in a memory. We should be the hero of our lives, not the victims of someone else's mistake...failure changes people, but so does success. Too many well intention persons get caught in the jingoistic repetitions of using the word black to depict badness, or social malaise. There is not much cultural continuity for slaves in a post slavery society; therefore they are bewildered in their social development. Most times Black societies, especially the Western ones are going through a steep learning curve in a hit and miss world that was conditioned to centuries of their human devaluation... perhaps this is one of the problems with Blacks and their persistent self hate. When Shadow refers to other similar form of human degradation as the **Osu cult-slave** that was abolished in 1956 by Eastern Nigerian Government. These people were slaves that were given to the Ibo people from other villages to compensate for "wrongs" done by their family. The Dread threw in the comment that although these unfortunates were the lowest of the society; they were feared because they were thought of as being watched over by the gods. What a comparison, freedom with fear! The Dread finally withholds his anger by dismissing Shadows by saying; "Shadows you are just an image of your real self at this time and space. Whenever you find your real self, and not just a mere shadow of yourself; then you and this I can communicate on a higher plane about the human communion with Melchizidek, this day." Well, it seems the Jah just power down the conversation and unceremoniously dismissed him. Shadows sees that the loquacious "Dread" is still nourishing the idea for the "back to Africa" quest. He still sees Africa as an earthly utopia. He had lived this long and never realized that the plights of colonial people were generally never well advertised. Brutal occurrences are prevalent to this day in many of the post colonial countries. Recently many people started thinking as little idiots by wishing for the *good old days*. Is this a refusal to growing up? Do they realize what comprises those olden days! The harsh conditions were always there, but children were shielded by their parents. He recalled a former President of Ghana chiding his people for still wanting to live in the Colonial past where every decision was made for them by the Colonialist Masters. He equated their behaviors to children refusing to grow up; still wanting to be living in their parent's home. The President should be less politically correct by saying "living in their slaver's house" after emancipation! But then the esteem President was too diplomatic to make such indelicate verbal comparison. It is now the time to seize the opportunities coming our way without awaiting handouts from overseas. Shadows remembers older people always telling about their missed opportunities in traveling to other places, or the knowledge of doing progressive things in their youth. On asking them why; you can observe the somber shadows on their face, and the chilliness in their demeanor while they made uncomfortable excuses how they were not really interested then ...their always, "If mi did want that, mi could a get it too." This is their ways of demeaning others accomplishments... Shadows too have grown up to recognize the results of misplaced priorities.

CHAPTER 20

HUMANITY

Shadows now looked at the decrepit railroad tracks populated with overgrown weeds as just another curiosity factor of past British Colonialism. In fairness to them, they did well, especially in keeping social order when compared to the present rulers who are latched into destructive partisan politics, only. Numerous social apologists are now excusing themselves by saying the former Colonialists have more financial resources, a longer history of ruling, or is it *tribal containment* than the present corrupt Black rulers. They are even stupidly saying the British killed more Black people than the present Black corrupt rulers…what a comparison! Anyway, the once mighty Empire too has faded into an historical curiosity, while staying afloat by riding their versatile cousin's coat tail, the Americans. Everyone does at this time; "so go where winners are!" He now looks at the worn tracks, recollecting his first train ride, a very short one with a very kind man, Mass Burty. Prior to that he remembers listening to his mother talking about the darkness of the Bog Walk tunnel; it was mystifying… He wanted to experience it! They alighted from one of those "halts" – train stops — dotting the Kingston to Port Antonio line. He usually looked at the passing train, and waved to the passengers; dreaming that one-day he would go wherever these people were coming from. Some unaware "grown ups" would chide him and his young friends for waving to the passengers by saying, "Dem a Black people like yourself. You fool, why are you waving to them?" The intonation here was they are poor people and do not merit your concern or adulation. Blacks were then identified with lack of power or merit. In those formative days, the Black uninspired masses were sowing the seeds of disrespect among their race. The "seven o'clock," early morning "diesel" to town was more for the socially advantaged "cool gentry" class persons to ride. He never recalls being chided for waving to them. The villagers' timetable was timed on the running of the trains at specific locations. "It is 10'clock, the train is coming!" Or, "It is after ten, because the train gone down already..." There were not many clocks around. Then again, some people have clocks, but could not tell the time. He remembers there was only one clock in the Village. Although many of the cultivators impressed their children to be on time for schools; the parents never seem to be hurrying any place except during the mornings if they worked the big landlords' farms. It seems that the big farmers were discipline people who expected their workers to be on time. On the other hand the teachers were extremely serious about punctuality. They have *ways* to make you comply!

The focal piece for the whole community was the Railway (JGR). An old "newspaper reading" lady once said the railroad was opened in 1845. The railway was considered a life line until the horrible Kendal Crash unleashed its carnage with numerous ghost stories of returning apparitions asking for directions to their homes. Shadows recollected his injured co-worker, a young man from that Crash who never seems to recover from a head wound. He became silent, sitting with sad eyes while avoiding eye contact, staring ahead in space as if inwardly weeping and viewing a sad replay. The Crash was a disaster waiting to happen because the coaches were very old. Then again, the indiscipline on the train was part of the general *outings mentality*. No wonder parents then were against their children going on school outings, although these were better managed. The general parental excuses were, "Mi hear some *pickney drownded* in the sea at an *outing...*" They could never tell you the name of the beach, the child's name or which school. Many parents used this tale as an economic excuse to disallow their children from going on a school *outing*. Even when the outing has nothing to do with the sea, these people would see the sea as a conflict. "Dem a fi pass the sea!" There were so many people whom do not know what the sea looks like, or what the other places of the island are like. Well, probably this situation has changed with the new available method of transportation in this "new age?" Everything has changed and not necessarily for the better...

Now the new radical trend of Globalization is built on consumerism...that unleashed a global technologically web that seems to impact freedom by controlling poorer countries: their privacy, stunting their social development, and deletion of age old ethnic cultures. A "big brother-like" control web that wants to micro-manage people but not to represent their social interests. Everything is merely business and the bottom-line of wishing on their theory that mass movement of goods perpetuates justice. Historically the NAZI (German) economy was strong, but where was the justice? The Black "Big Wigs" in charge, at least they think so…but on the international scene we are as important as foraging little *sprats* roaming the oceans with the great *whites*. Just ask the people of the Jewish faith how they felt with no local representation during those dark and turbulent days before the existence of the Israeli country. Little countries are suffering a loss of identity. Globalization controls individuals and communities (villages) with their influx of cheaper mass-produced foreign goods and services; thereby destroying community with emerging businesses. There can be no favorable competition for local goods when there is unfair competition with the global giants. Economic strangulation arises when little countries are forced in signing international treaties, which require them to fiercely cut each others throat just to survive. If you don't like the *global* edict, there are always legal tribunals where "small sprats" can appeal, but have you ever noticed the decisions are always in favor of the powerful "great whites." Why not; they set up these new constricting mumbo-jumbo courts, with their complicated "*long arguments*" at The Hague (or elsewhere) to hang struggling little countries' interests. While in the background the "G-numeric" countries conspired with their shifty financial "prescriptions" with crushing International debts to hurt social transformation (growth). During this constricting period the local creative business acumen is stultified as their little emerging businesses try competing not within their local village communities but on the global scale. The result: social decay, mass unemployment, illiteracy, anger and finally lawlessness. The same old vision of using force to control the population after corrupting the young is prevalent among Black nations of post chattel slavery society. Whenever they cannot deliver on their political promises, they resort to the usage of passing draconian laws and then using brutal police tactics to kill the younger males, especially. It seems this will solve their sexual problems, but not the social ones... There are indications that the politicos think it is better to *warehoused* than to seek a cure. So far it seems that executions have not solved their problems. The concept, if they are having some fun, then finds a way for taxing it, or criminalizes it, is their usual response to freedom. This always seems to be the way of all conservatives. It is like saying if they read their Bible and feel happy and started praising God, then brand them as heretics and then kill them. The business minded robed religious elites did this before; do you remember? Take the case of ganja decriminalization and the global interference; why build prisons to incarcerate people for smoking a spliff cigar, or saying the "rass" word? If the answer to the latter is that the whites usually do it; then were they always right? Is this where we again generally excuse our behaviors by alluding that the whites may have removed their physical chains, but they still physically control us with their brains (or is it their skin color)? Slavery was correct then! No wonder your CARICOM is dumb about reparation in Durham. How many persons are you going to still imprisoned before coming to an amicable conclusion? The preachers here display no sympathy unless you put a TV microphone in their face. They see the people's needs as simple *skin effect* satisfaction that is outside the scope of spiritual vibrancy.

Poverty does not necessarily produce only failure. It can also condition the mind to live and possible excels...the human spirit is indefinable. Everyone wants to be a privileged person. We cannot continue using incarceration and death to fight poverty. Resistance is associated with force. Childhood brutality can be a root cause for criminality. Now some sociologist are saying you have too many unwanted children from young single parents, "baby mothers" without father figures; a result of the messages from your indiscipline dance-hall music craze. But then your economy thrives on this type of fun... Your trying to setup a predominantly Black-staffed Caribbean kangaroo legal court to swiftly try and execute poor Black men is not the answer to your social problem. Oh, yes, we already know it will be for poor Black people. How many rich whites, or rich Blacks or other races ever get executed? The removal of a single person's freedom has a domino effect. Using judicial expediency or class prejudice against the fatherless poor Black ghetto victims relative to the Upper St. Andrew BMW-driving victorious elites will not get you peace behind your grilled homes. We have to acknowledge that Black groups of victor and victim actually, *"Dem no plant gungo a line!"* Should we now ask, "Who is next?" We have transcend the simple confrontation of a scared country boy in an old cemetery, silently pleading for his live as irate higglers haggle over his life, with their sharp blades near his throat. The nation crying for mercy or defensively screaming "murder" is no longer just a hysterical mother wailing for her family; now it is the country screaming, and seeking a reprieve from violence... It seems police action is now too late to help; therefore we all weep together. Our years of little divisive *"licky licky"* policy finally worms its way through out our lackadaisical society. Does the "colonial model" of governance still work? It seems our world grew smaller and we can now easily *"reach out and touch others."* Alas! But no one wants to touch us anymore; as shown by the hardened attitudes of our formerly friendly industrial *global villagers* new operational desires to enact *"visa barriers"* against us as clinical defenses against our numerous *"mules"* and their unseen, but well connected confederates in high places. If we are all from the same *yard*, then the innocent will have to suffer with the guilty: "If mi can't catch quaku mi ketch him shut!"—if I cannot catch you, then I will catch (damage) your interests.

With this type of evolution we cannot easily use disinformation to hide our sins. We are all closely linked, so blatantly murdering our young Black male citizens may not be the way to go as a form of population control. And we are actually showing the world that their treatment towards us was justified...giving credence that Blacks cannot govern as shown by the Black nations in Africa. No wonder some of the media's hazy minded intellectual wonders are espousing the lame view that the Black masses benefited from slavery! Do you think these idiots were looking back over time at the tribulation that befalls the race, the individuals, at their very parents caught in the acts? Were these media people quantifying the misery that brought them here by counting the rapes of their mothers and the castration of their father as a condition to their so-called Western freedom? How many of their parents have to be shipped, whipped, raped, and excruciatingly tortured by the "pale pigmented" Marquis de Sade-type people before we are qualified for a Western freedom? In looking back over time, do you think their anguish cries were like pigs being stuck with a butcher's knife? Can anyone hear the anguish screams of "Murder! Murder!" that ends in silence; even until this day when our guardian, CARICOM remains unconscionable deaf! Makes you still proud of your "genetic" benefits? Perhaps most of us would rather shout, "Please leave dear old mom and dad...we will seek our *benefits* in another global direction." Oh! Less we forget; what shade are those who espoused the benefits of slavery for the Black masses on this Western island?

Perhaps we have been listening to far too many rabble rousers throughout the ages, from the village preachers to the national politicians. Now the modern media types are trying our patience as they hyped new sensationalism to continually keep their names on the front pages. As the older village women would have said, "dem a cut dem eye at us and throw dem '*casm* pon we!" Imagine suggesting things like *slavery was beneficial to the (poor) Blacks*! Irrespective of which values hyped; whether secular, spiritual, modern or traditional; we are still living in a catch (grab) as you can atmosphere. This is primarily so because we are only adept in dealing in words but not with actions. We are no longer afraid of new words because the Internet is upon us; now we are afraid to use new ideas. Or, probably we are just plainly too lazy to compete. It seems that our history of not being informed have finally caught up with us! But that is an unfair assumption, because we wanted information, and had fought hard for it too. If you don't believe that; then check the attitude and the pain in the demeanor of one of those illiterate district "newspaper buyers" as he tactfully asked a child to read to him on one of those secluded areas on a winding path. Check the sparkle in his eyes as you tell him what's going on…listen to his breathing, and watched the relaxation of his jaws. Is it likely our politicians "chat too much," and our sleazy religious leaders are still chiding us to close our eyes to reality; telling us that our request for a better spiritual understanding is "flying in God's face?" Are we viewing ourselves through different prisms that reflect the worst part of our African tribal heritage in dealing with social conflict? Shadow is reminded of the incident when a young woman asked an uppity civil servant a question. The civil servant repeated her answer, but the poor girl could not understand her. Eventually the civil servant picks up the telephone and handed it to the villager saying, "It's for you. Your Village called saying their idiot is missing." Sometimes information is very hard to get and then decipher… It seems we now have the information, but are unable to decipher and implement its content for our benefits.

Should we now ask the question, "What do you want, advancement or ignorance?" We are products of the usual dismissive remarks, "…flying into God's face…" and the general excuse of "…mi a Christian," but those are just utterances as the old Rasta usually say. If we are such a Christian nation how come we killed so many of our own people! Are we living in accordance to the Christian religion, which is "credited" with killing the most people in the world during The Christian Crusades, the American Civil War, and World Wars 1 & 2? Perhaps its time to say Shibboleth and cross over to a newer way by tapping into the creative process and invoke the Creators' will; while stepping away from the conformed, well-suited and uniformed church chaplains with only their book learning. It seems that the unschooled grass roots preacher of yester-year has taken us this far, but the well-educated and expensively attired contemporaries cannot spiritually do any better! They all "talked" togetherness because they are of the same religion, but they generally practiced divisiveness...my robe is different, more expensive and has a better color coordination than yours, Praise God! Then they resisted helping others that are not of the same congregation, and are not their friends and family. Is this similar to saying: I will take garrison A with politico X, you take garrison B with politico Y, and never the twain shall meet? A very similar action as the Catholic organization did in dividing the World into two spheres of influences centuries ago...using their un-deciphered politico-Christianity with its lack of spirituality, and unwillingness to recognize the Blacks as humans.

The rampant cronyism that stifles social progress has numerous dark skinned people playing the waiting game to get on the economic train of opportunity, while scrutinizing the status and performance of their *Brer Nancy* and *Brer Tucumbat* political parties with their politics of intimidation and death... There is no patriotism, just political partisanship, yes. Where people were first unruly at the movie theatres, now they are murderous in the everyday walk of life. The Buff's "street mentality" is now the order of the day within all facet of the society. Let's digress here, and rectify this Buff's comparison. Buff was cool, and certainly no fool or buffoon, but he was not the selected leadership type we voted for. The social operational theatre here has more divisions of social seating than in Buff's old simple class conscious movie house. These "divisions" are infested by deadly and greedy tribal garrisons that answer to no one except the Overlord with bigger guns. The legacy of the old minute village secrecy and a zest for privacy seems to have given rise to dark government secrecy, which breeds open conflict and injustice. In years gone by, the asking of certain questions could get a young person in trouble. There were always the repeated, "What you want to do, fly in a God's face!" This was not a question; it was a threat; just watch the face and observe the body language. Those times were definitely not the information age. But in this age of information, openness and accountability are not the order of the day for many island governments. Everything is still secretive. To openly question the politicians could definitely get the citizens killed.

As everyone seeks modern toys in this latter day concept of the consumerism renaissance called Globalization; the question is: "Where is our humanity going during our quest for this modernization?" Shadows remembered a more cooperative neighborhood where young men and boys in the cold mornings would push start the only car in the district.

This was a raggedy older car that has a low battery voltage or whatever. It seems that it would start whenever the sun rises. It became the district's spectacle and point of argument if anyone believes the car would start tomorrow morning. Shadows could hear the activities with joyous voices shouting, "It's starting now man; you hear it!" Those were the days when technology and science were just dreams for the population. There were those who could not even patch their own bicycle inner tube when it is punctured…they just did not have the knowledge, and no one was willing to train them. Shadows recalls asking his mother why they bother pushing the car. She replied, "We need to help other people. If you are sick in the night he may help you!" Some weeks later this same man took his mom to town in the early morning when she missed the diesel. This was not the modern time, so getting sick during the night was a very bad scene. They would have to saddle up the mules and cart with a bumpy ride on iron wheeled carts. If the ride didn't help kill you; then the sickness may! Then there were not many doctors. Of course there were those villagers with their medicinal concoction of the "preserved scorpion in a rum bottle" who would swear that it works for pains, especially arthritis or rheumatism. We have to remember that was long before the modern biotech "wish list" and stem cell research with their "friendly" pharmaceutical buddies doing their active-cell-site re-alignment. Anyway, these district masseuse or masseur was not the occultist or Obeah "dabblers in the clandestine arts" types. Bear in mind that the cautious and sometimes crafty villagers do not like to be physically touched by these "dabblers," especially during the nights. Ever heard the stinging cultural reprimand: "Mi no know where your hand a come from; so don't touch me!" The crafty and superstitious villager may have had a very private business transaction with the "dabbler" and perhaps even blame him for his sickness... believing his enemy had "boomerang" or did a "return blow" on him. Perhaps he did not finish paying the "dabbler" also...so many little scenarios here. Just be reminded that no one ever dies in these villages of natural causes; they are always believed to be killed by someone. No, they are not talking about the natural terminating force of *Death* doing the killing; it has to be some friend or a "stray blow," meaning it was not intended for you but you were in the way at the wrong time. Anyway, the village "massagers" were of the nurturing herbalist group that you would call during the nights when your pain kept you awake and groaning for "days and extra days." Be reminded that no well thinking "dabbler" in those days (or night!) would be seen playing with dead scorpion in some restricted receptacle like a bottle. From information gathered; we may not say the same about their affinity for a dead human body! In those days the term "witchdoctor" was irrelevant, and was never mentioned. All things African were totally culturally "whitewashed," except for the physical features that could not be easily altered, hence the residual legacy of our shame for most of our ancestry. The mind got warped (or attuned or "British-ed?") but the body reminds us of our true parents. Ever think we were well inculcated to dislike ourselves as a group? Someone said, *"If they grab your mind the body has no chance but to follow or die."* Trust an astute and business-minded Americans to notice this mind-body connection as just another interfacing business niche to exploit. It seems that most of our social and religious energy is spent smoothing the transition of our "follow or die" interface. This is where the religious preachers and the social police face off, while using our mind (and, or body) as puck in their institutional hockey game as they force us to negotiate the social turnstiles on our "free way" of life.

Shadows first encounter with a "doctor" was during his visit to a dispenser who used a *red towel* on his chest, not a stethoscope... There were many stories about this piece of cloth, eliciting the usual respectful discourse... *"him a high man* you know!" The dispenser told him his *grinder* was not working properly...what a patronizing usage of words. He gave him a pint of medicine in a cream soda bottle that helped. In those days, yes, BYOMB; *bring your own medicine bottle.* If you didn't then you will have to buy an "aerated water," – a pop – to get the empty bottle; an extra budget you did not plan on! On the other hand it was the first time Shadows had ever seen a woman outrageously bossing around a man. The doctor's wife acted like a shrill noisy siren, always bossing around everyone in sight. One groaning older patient caustically referred to the wife's behavior towards her quiet husband as an "uneven yoke." The technical knowledge base during those times was very limited because the rulers wanted it so. Now we have a broader base but we seem to have less cooperation in this modern time. We shall not get into demographics and social behavioral patterns here; we just need to use good old common sense thing and "know you self" as the old Jahs usually say. We better unyoke our senses from tribalism and other disruptive fallacy. It seems that our progress lies in expanding our consciousness; of not being controlled by the old pigmentation edict, or believing in the vision of a non-Black skin means economic and social power...

We should really question what does the term Modernization means? Does it mean Americanization to the guys in the rural and urban areas who watched all these televised happy beer party commercials and abundance of other goods beamed into their homes? It seems nothing "home grown" is ever worthwhile when compared to the newly "import America!" Shadows recalls long ago his mom refusing to buy local made cocoa, which she implied tasted like mud; the result of an old colonial plot to keep quality products from being manufactured in the islands. Everyone wants what seems to be uncontrolled spending, but no one wants the stress of balancing the checkbook after being constantly pressured to buy something new. Are we all bowing to secularism with its "moneyed" Christianity of fooling people with their politically inspired prayers? This attitude seems to work well for the Americans, but not for others. Perhaps this shows the Island Christianity needs a different approach. The island's politically inspired "prayer meetings" seem to be ineffective so far in stemming the tide of violence. It appears that the new Americanized religious macro-management is ineffective on the island. Has the district *balm yards* and *wrapped head preachers* no longer effective? The murders and mayhem still continues. What are the secular differences between the USA and the Island governments? We both have disoriented youths, prominently listed as males. On the island they are *standing* in Jamaica and *breathing* everything American...they actually show little respect for their country. Then how could they; they were brutalized from birth throughout their childhood by a system that is socially stagnant, repressive, economically retarded with untold social irresponsibility. Do the grass roots groups in the small Churches help each other as in olden days? Today, we are not expecting an illiterate parson repeating scriptures with emphasis on texts that are read to him, but if he can help he would be certainly welcome. There are streams of continual promises as politics and crime hog the media. At this time they both seem to be the same thing. We have words and ideas which seem to deform society and distort the truth. We understand the immediacy of prayers and affirmations are generally not quickly observed, except in a miraculous form, but there is still a need for spiritual renewal. We need to emerge with a new mindset to blossom anew and be flooded with positive circumstances that calls for a new spiritual approach to justice and truth. If we want our lives to reflect our inner awareness, our *rainbow covenant* with reality cannot be some scary childish physical aberration under some dim bridge. It is time we straightened our resolve, and change the shape and the symbolic blight of the grim Reaper's question-mark scythe into a robust straight exclamation mark of enchantment.

Perhaps the Church can help us align our minds with the divine code of Spiritual awareness. But in its search for Earthly power over the disadvantaged masses, it appears the Church has left us in ignorance, looking up into the sky at jet planes; aimlessly muttering, "Mi nah do nothing because *God soon come fi him world,"* while they continually get drunk on the ceremonial wine of earthly power. Here again, the sad irony is most wrongdoers seem to be going around quoting Biblical passages whenever they are prosecuted; or whenever they are seeking political offices. Quoting these passages merely reflects who selected the passages rather than their Christian beliefs. As a child, Shadows listened to some of the most outrageous Psalms, and even then he promised to avoid praying for others destruction, (or ignorantly calling a *brother* a harlot!) We need renewal and recollection and not the unjust labeling of the Master's creation as criminals because their social circumstances betrayed their spiritual growth. We should give help for the joy of giving, with no restriction and the popular clamoring for a red-dressed Santa Claus-media exposure... at the end of our offering.

The primary or elementary school mindset of flaying away in the primary political schoolyard has to be changed. Are we still looking for a merciful referee to stop the beating? Imagine, at this time we are still debating if Primary education and Pre-Primary education should be free in the Bill of Rights. Some of us, many of us too, ate *bulla cake, or flaun flaun, or fried dumplings out of glass case* or in the earlier days "shut pan" while attending a free elementary or primary school. Do we need free education like the UK and the US...it about time we debunk the myth that we can live without it. The simplistic "lead cow-head" days were yesteryear labor affairs. We cannot impress anyone by just sitting on a rural embankment digesting our nicotine fix, and appears to be happy! Doing such again, is failing to help the very young…retrogression! Is this an era when the African chiefs resisted sending their young masses to school when the Europeans presented the occasion? Is the logic to "Keep them foolish and you will always stay in power!" not a step towards chaos? Nationally we are still substituting cruel partisanship politics for truth, justice and progress.

The former political directives spanning the last 50 years were to blindly substitute Cold War economic ideologies (or rhetoric) at the expense of nourishing the Garvey's doctrine of Black respect and self-reliance. It seems the new "well learned ones" have accepted the jaundiced attitude of Free Market collusion in accepting the quiescent state of preaching racial diversity because they have no moral courage to go their own way with the Garvey's self reliance concept. People are now looking far beyond the shifty and murky forlorn faces of these political strategists and recognize their confused and foolish state of denials. The result is indicative of their venomous political example of disunity; a legacy of strife and destruction of never in agreement on worthwhile issues. It seems the progenitors of the Elmina Castle survived the brutal Middle Passage only to create the most despicable Western Black tribal and class prejudices society! Think some of those African witchdoctors foresaw this, and that is why they got rid of our dear old mom and dad from the ancestral land?

"Woe, the bones show a disturbance coming from your children…"

Our motivational concept should be focusing on a more sophisticated method of governing, and get away from the same old primary school mindset of the *"bruk a big baton"* over someone's head as were scripted by their former intimidating colonial masters. The Masters could do that and get away because they intelligently kept weapons away from the poor. Look back over our history and recall that whenever the "management" gave their big muscled "rhygins" guns the rangers were prone to commit murders. The location and time has changed but it seems the ineptitude, which results in mismanagement, has already had its commands indelibility scorched within the genes. At least it seems so! The present rulers are seeing money as the only clinical component to progress. We need to identify problems, not to just understand the information, but to use it for a progressive change. The generation should be educated to differentiate between *freedom* and *freeness*. If you are on a quest for freeness; you may get a "free gift" to take you to your grave as in 1754-1767 when the British forces in North America distributed tainted smallpox blankets to the unaffected Native American tribes. It could have been given with the best interest at heart. (*Whose?*) Is this some bio-weapon or what! So just be careful who is giving the gifts. Better use common sense and drink some "search me heart"–bush tea— first, then ask (yourself) what the donor wants before accepting the gift. It seems our Black "tribe(s)" on the island needs no donor of death, not even the HIV/AIDS epidemic to wipe them out; they already have the self hate, ballistic weapons coupled with their ignorance, greed and corruption in high places.

"How can they win with the things they are using!"

Sometimes we have to review the past to learn (study) lessons (designs) for the future. We now question: "What is the prerequisite to peace?" To minimize aggression we definitely should have justice and the removal of social disenfranchisement that lead to contentions. These are the conditions that generates the belief that "...*wherever Blacks go they bring trouble.*" (Sorry older folks, Shadows have to disagree with you here!) Poor people are too vulnerable to injustice, even more so now than when they were under the old colonial system. They are more so now, because there are more of them with dwindling resources and the disproportionate distribution of wealth (resources). The society is more at risks because they now have guns and are willing to use them; "*dem nuh skin up,*" nor "*in a any long arguments!*" because they never had anything, and therefore have nothing to lose. Is it better to be aggressive and die than being docile, and exist as everyone's footstool? Their young lives were generally one of brutality so they have no human compassion for anyone. Yes, "*dem a shoot, dem a loot, dem a wail...!*" as the once upon a time saying goes. The positive emphasis of the old or the new social security of the family village was never there for them. The explicitness of the new "*dance hall*" music sexual exploitation was always there though, with its disrespect for motherhood and other positively entrenched social values. In the old village community the invisible Colonial "*dem will haul and pull you*"— government was a faceless deterrent, but now the media-hyping "*them*" is inconsequential when a helpless child cries. They gave no parental oversight to parenting, but quickly act as a group of howling jackals or a flock of "sniffing" John Crows fussing over choice spots during a carrion feast when challenged by a Parson John Crow; crying, "Hang them!" when these same unsupervised young disadvantaged people committed crimes. The Europeans and also the Rastafarians seem to understand the saying: "If you do not protect the young your society will eventually perish." (Imagine grouping these two diametrically opposed groups together as one beneficial package?) Perhaps we could emphasize the family along the lines of good parentage within the new village life. Where is the governmental oversight for the treatment of the young! The vibrant and spiritual Rastas are still there but so are the trendy Dreadlocks articulating their "dance hall" popularity based on crassness and promiscuity. Yes, sex sells! The dance-hall DJs are the product of their society, the lower society. If they did not make a living this way, they may become just another statistics for the unfeeling system. They are a defining force for the coming generation in showing that money and power; (both may be the same thing) are the parameters for popularity, but not necessarily for tranquility. The DJs are being used by the commercial class to attract money to the island, as did the old reggae giants did years ago. Their crassness is a commercial by-product of their type of music. They have no other means of earning a living, and are generally not trained for anything else. Now the entrepreneurs who helped put them on a pedestal are complaining because of political heat. Have we forgotten that everyone here *openly* expressed their freedom in the accepted reality of openly living with iron bars on the windows of their beautiful homes, high on the hill tops (and now without their gramophones...)

The "village support connection" or the "neighborhood district support system" is a traditional support system that is now considered quaint. It seems that a new and fiercer type of "village" support structure is now entrenched in the Big City urban areas, and is cautiously spreading its tentacles towards the government's "cash cow," the tourist areas! These *structures* are now referred to as "garrisons." It is speculated that the garrisons groups arises for the same reason as the older district groups; because those that governed had abandoned their responsibilities to the poorer people. Although the Spaniards gave up Jamaica in 1664 (according to the history book, but who wrote it anyway), the leader of these social groups are referred to with the Spanish nobility name "don." Someone said the ones called "dons" have no relationship to Don Arnoldo De Yssassi the last governor of Jamaica. Neither are they Sicilians. Others claimed the tribal *dons* are searching the Duke of Albermarle's old slave records in England to determine their tribal linkage... (Think "The Alb" got a Royal Warrants to capture and transport some of *dem* slaves in Africa? Disturbing eh, but why? Still wondering if the Warrants are still legal; just waiting for the next round of the Royal visitation?) It is rumored that the requirements for being a *don* doesn't necessarily includes the knowledge of the Spanish, or the Italian language. Some people are still wondering, "What is the resume for being a "don?" What is their mission statement?" Ever think about asking the island Parliamentarians?

Shadows recalling that Jah Rabi the One-I, while watching the numerous crouching Black bodies toiling in a cane field quipped, that the unconscionable governing Europeans may have had the general feeling we were an island of little Black animals that could not help themselves because our minds were still in the baby state of human development....a type of human Darwinian development. His mom earlier usual comment whenever some Black person acted silly was, "Slavery come and gone, and Black people are still in darkness." Now, Shadows is wondering what the governing Black faces think. Are these two statements fair assessments of their opinions of the disadvantaged masses? We are on the world stage now, so this is not some schoolboy deliberately muffing his line at grandma's little church play. We have signed international agreements so we have to produce whether *we plant gungo a line*, —being neighborly or not. In other words, whether you *"have dem up in a you stomach"* – having a grudge or not, you better *"skin up wid them,"*—smile with them and play by their rules. The rule of life predicts that death follows birth, or night follows day, (or vice-versa). As the night drew nearer Shadows realizes that his old world was coming to an end. His old family and relatives, except one are no longer here. During the night, unknown to him, he was watching his loving Auntie, the last matriarch of the family taking her last laborious breath. It was an unrecognized finality of their human connection. It brought back memories of viewing his mother's final moment through an impersonal and curtained hospital window. "He thinks about a meeting somewhere, far beyond the clouds and sky and a welcoming voice saying, "Sister you stay *out there* very long, now welcome home…" The moment returned him to an innocent era when his mother took him to his first fair. Yes! No Briton was there. They would consider their attendance as a violation of their social order; socializing where these *"jumped up Colonials"* gawking at a hand turned Ferris wheel near a bloody cow pasture…bloody Dickens I say dear fellow! It was Shadows first social gathering, and the first he had ever been outside during the nights. No! No *rolling calf or duppy* was seen there, silly. The fair had a primitive hand turned Ferris wheel. Then as now, he refused to go on the strange rotating contraption. He now believes it was during the Christmas season. People were dressed in "clean clothes"—well attired —and everyone was having fun. There were numerous vendors with glass cases selling cakes, "drops,"— coconut cakes and other candies. It was the first time he saw a person smoking cigarettes; the strange flaming, poisonous white sticks, attached to their lips. He hazily remembers the strange crowd and the place being brilliantly lit by gas-lanterns. He stood there with an invigorating feeling of doing something differently; like enjoying the joyous outdoor freedom as a part of reinventing himself in sustaining his young vibrant inner fire.

Shadows believes it is not feasible to go back to those days, but it typifies his desire for inner calm…that fair was an affair of the heart like the cyclic motion of the wheel renewing its position in time and space. He may never play ball on a busy school road again and experience his young awakened passion. But he can love the memory and continually replay it, and laugh at the irate motorists, who he knows will always look out for his welfare, and warn him of impending danger by saying, "Boy come out a de road! You foolish…?" Perhaps, just perhaps, it is now our times to come away from imminent danger and be like the watchful motorists looking out for our young playful ones… Guidance!

About the Author

I live in California, in the heart of the Silicon Valley where cutting edge technology rules. I am from the Caribbean and still visit the calmness of the warm Caribbean Sea. *Time Curtain* is my third book. My first book is *Cyber Trek,* which light heartedly deals with the problems of Caribbean migrants in the industrial centers in North America and Europe.

I also like writing science fiction. *Oneness in a Cocoon,* my second book, and *Trees,* my fourth book are science fiction.